SUSSEX BEACH TRADES
Sea Coal to Trippers

Michael Langley

 Middleton Press

Front cover pictures:
 top left - see caption no. 8
 top right - see caption no. 38
 lower left - see caption no. 91
 lower right - see caption no. 106

Back cover pictures:
 top - see caption no. 112
 bottom - see caption no. 113

About the Author-

An early interest in photography, coastal shipping and the harbours of Sussex would lead to a career in deep sea shipping with the P&O Group culminating in Ship Management. A later move to the Isle of Wight saw a return to the original interests resulting in research and publication of a number of local history style shipping books for the areas from Kent to Cornwall.

Published August 2010

ISBN 978 1 906008 80 2

© Middleton Press, 2010

Design Deborah Esher

Published by
 Middleton Press
 Easebourne Lane
 Midhurst
 West Sussex
 GU29 9AZ
Tel: 01730 813169
Fax: 01730 812601
Email: info@middletonpress.co.uk
www.middletonpress.co.uk

Printed in the United Kingdom by Henry Ling Limited, at the Dorset Press, Dorchester, DT1 1HD

CONTENTS

	Page
Glossary & Abbreviations	4
Introduction	6
General Map	6

1. Medieval harbours — 9
   - The Cinque Ports
   - Old Customs boundaries
   - Storm damage and effects

2. Ship and boat construction — 34
   - Clinker built types
   - Trading ships
   - Hastings beach built

3. Beach sailing yachts and tripper boats — 48

4. Piers, paddle steamers & promenading — 58
   - Development of excursions
   - Piers - history at the resorts

5. Beach handled cargoes - non coal — 65
   - Chalk, lime, flints/boulders
   - General goods, coastwise, etc.

6. Smuggling — 72
   - That other old beach 'trade'

7. The arrival of the Railways — 92
   - Effects on road transport
   - Coastal cargo movement
   - Freedom of individuals
   - Start of the tripper market

8. The long 'reign' of coal — 109
   - Origins of coal by sea
   - North East coast exports
   - Sussex consumption
   - Beaches, harbours, ships

9. Seaside health benefits — 141
   - Resort origins

10. Proposed harbour schemes — 149
    - Modern marinas

Appendicies

I	Sussex beach built vessels extant 1873	152
II	Sussex registered vessels extant "	153
III	Trading areas for Sussex ships "	154
IV	Sailing rigs on the Sussex coast (1800-1900)	155

Bibliography	156
Index	157
Acknowledgements	159
Photographic sources	159

MAPS

1. Rye Bay	8
2. Hastings area	15
3. Pevensey to Eastbourne	40
4. Eastbourne to Birling Gap	45
5. Cuckmere Haven to Newhaven	73
6. Brighthelmstone to Southwick (early)	86
7. Brighton to Southwick (later)	86
8. River Adur Estuary	108
9. Worthing	124
10. Littlehampton – Arundel	132
11. Bognor Regis	140
12. Selsea and Pagham Harbour (early)	147
13. Selsey and Pagham Harbour (later)	148

PREFACE

The carriage of coal by sea to Sussex had grown at a moderate pace for centuries. Arrival of the industrial revolution witnessed a rapid expansion of the coal trade and the sudden appearance of the local railway network in the mid 1800s would bring a hitherto undreamed of freedom of movement for the public at large. The resorts soon flourished to provide entertainment and accommodation for the new breed of intrepid trippers. Entrepreneurs soon developed amusements and pastimes such as piers, paddle steamer excursions and boat trips to occupy their time. This book aims to take a specific look at the growth, peak and demise of the coal trade, other beach handled trades, and how the tripper market evolved into modern tourism and the holiday industry. Images drawn from the early 1800s to 2010 help illustrate the ever changing Sussex coastal scene.

GLOSSARY & ABBREVIATIONS

MB   Motor Boat   MV   Motor Vessel   PS   Paddle Steamer
SL   Steam Launch   SS   Steam Ship

Tonnages:
Gross Registered Tonnage, abbr. grt; g, volumetric measure of all enclosed space applied to all ships. 100cu.ft = 1 gross ton. True indicator of a ship's overall physical size.

Net Registered Tonnage, abbr. nrt, n, sometimes referred to as just registered tonnage. Derivation from sailing ship days in the wine trade when a 'tun' * implied a wine barrel of 252 gallons capacity. The number of such barrels gave an indication of earning volume.
* Wine tun decreed to be 252 gallons by Act in 1423.

Deadweight Tonnage, abbr. dwt, d, the actual weight carrying capacity of the ship in tons, including fuel, water, stores etc, plus cargo.

Tons 'burthen' or 'burden' were statements of deadweight used for cargo ships in the 17th and 18th centuries.

Knots/kts, Speed in nautical miles (6,080ft) per hour.

Spring Tides: Fortnightly periods of greater tidal range – 'higher' high water and 'lower' low water.
Neap Tides;   Intervening periods of lesser tidal range – 'lower' high water and 'higher' low water.

Littoral Drift: Eastward movement of shingle along the Channel shoreline.

Some early commodity measures- volumetric:
Heaped or dry, ie; in the corn trade:
One Chaldron = 35 Bushels = 12 Sacks. [1.3m3 or 1300litres modern, or 35.32cu.ft] Chaldron also deemed to be approx. 28cwt.
One Bushel = 4Pecks = or 8Gallons.
One Sack = 3Bushels = 24Gallons

Stowage Factors: (typical values dependent on grade and moisture content.
Coal: 40-50cu.ft./ton
Chalk: 36-40   "
Shingle: 23   "
Gravel: 21   "
Sand: 19   "
Timber: English Oak 43cu.ft/ton
          An early timber measure was the 'load' stowing at:
          For unhewn timber 40cu.ft/ton
          For hewn timber   50cu.ft/ton
          A load equalled approx 1.25 tons modern.

DEFINITIONS

Sea coal: arch; originally coal brought from Newcastle by sea.   tpa: tons per annum.

Whip: light derrick with tackle for hoisting

Gin: Tackle block with hoisting rope(s), bell ends, to be simultaneously hauled upon.

Coal Whipper: Man, powering device for raising coal from a ship's hold.

Tripper: Person who goes on a trip, especially for a day, to the seaside or other resort.

Clinker built: Boat hulls built of over lapping planks 'clenched' with copper nails.

Sailing Vessels:
- Smack: Historical term describing small single masted trading or fishing vessels.
- Sloop: As above fore and aft rig usually one head sail. Gaff rigged
- Cutter: As above with two head sails and a running bowsprit, also gaff rigged.
- Lugger: Two or three masted vessel with four cornered sails usually used for fishing. The central mast was made redundant by the mid 1800s. Large versions of luggers had been used by Smugglers and the Royal Navy.
- Yawl: Small fishing or trading vessel with a small mizzen mast stepped abaft the rudder post. Gaff rigged.
- Ketch: Larger trading or fishing types with much bigger mizzen mast forward of the rudder post, compared to the yawl. Gaff rigged.
- Schooner: Trading vessels with two, three or more masts, fore and aft rigged. They often carried square topsails on the foremast only. Usually gaff rigged.
- Brig: Two masted square rigged trading vessel.
- Snow: As per the brig but carried a small extra mast abaft the mainmast for the 'spanker' sail.
- Brigantine: As per the brig but square rigged on foremast only, fore and aft on the mainmast. This was more economic on man power.
- Barque: Larger square rigged trading vessel. If square rigged on all masts known as 'a full rigged ship'.
- Barquentine: Square rigged on foremast only, fore and aft on others.

Early Shipping Records:

1760s   Lloyds Registers commenced and added ever greater detail of ships and their rigs up until
1863   Subsequently all British and, where known, foreign vessels of sail, steam and motor propulsion have been included but generally of craft exceeding 100 tons size.
1857   Mercantile Navy Lists commenced. All British and Commonwealth unpowered and powered craft right down to 3-4 tons size included. Ceased publication in 1976.

INTRODUCTION

Sea coal and Trippers may initially seem to be somewhat unrelated with but very little in common. However, it would be general industrial growth and the increasing demand for coal that would ultimately release a previously static population to the joys of travel. The freedom of movement we are so accustomed to today was unleashed in the mid 1800s by steam ships and steam railways. Coal had been shipped South from Newcastle for centuries in modestly growing quantities, long before the industrial revolution took hold. Once manufacturing industries acquired steam power, coal demand burgeoned. Arrival in the early 1800s of local town gas generation and a century later of electricity generating stations would further accelerate consumption drastically. Coal would reign 'king' until the changeover to oil fuel began in the mid 20th century, to be further diminished by nuclear power's arrival in the second half of the century. By the 1970s North Sea gas supply had ended land based gas production from coal. Today a considerable percentage of electricity is generated using gas fired plant. Additionally, domestic coal fires have become a rarity, further reducing coal demand.

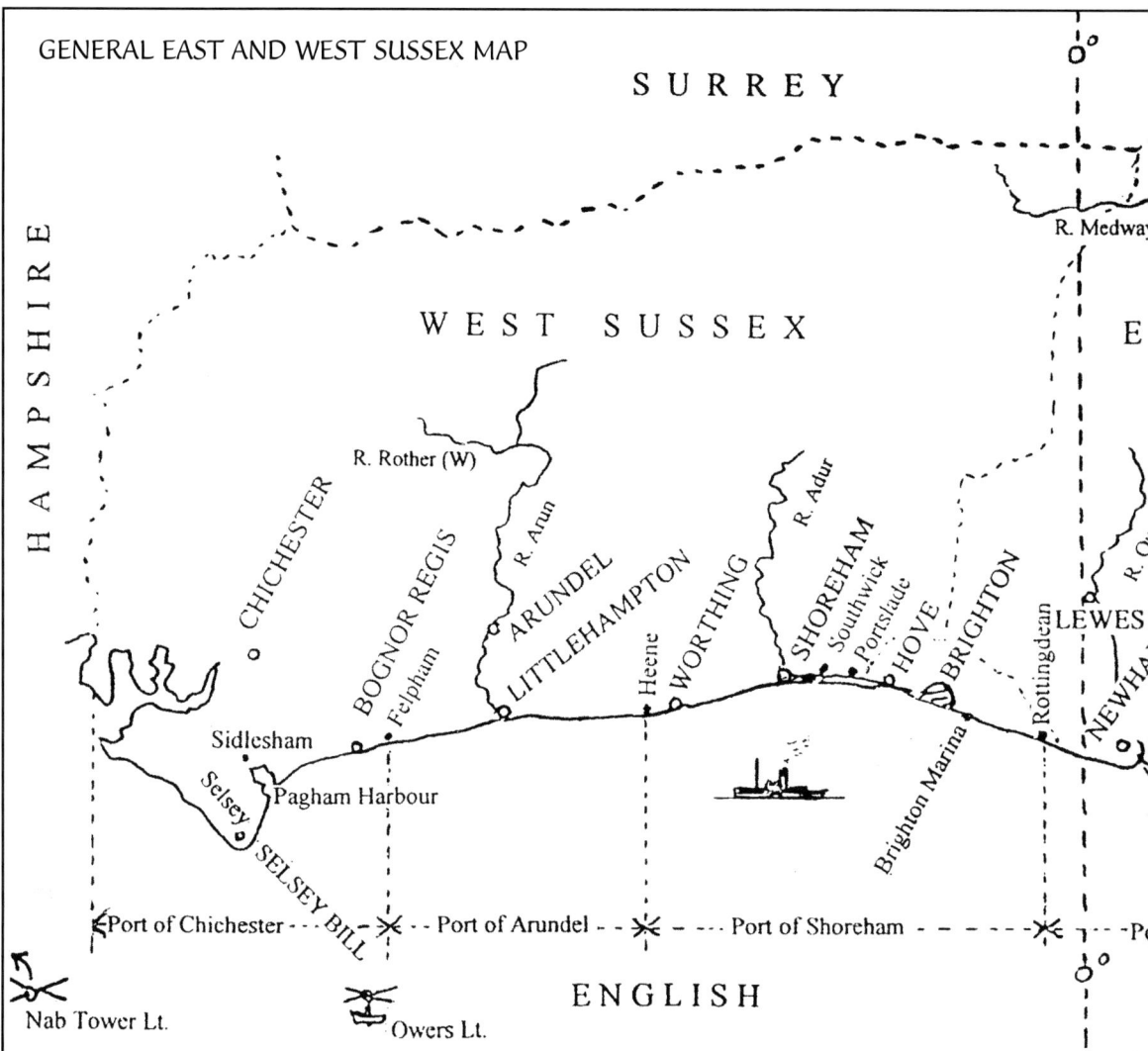

Coastal resorts grew in popularity from the mid 1700s as some consideration began to be given to the nation's health and well being. Traditional inland spa resorts realised they now had competition. Many of the seaside resorts simply developed out of existing fishing hamlets, others materialised on what would today be called green field sites. By 1800 many resorts were deemed to be fashionable places to take the waters and Royal patronage helped considerably. However they existed mainly for the elite and affluent until the coming of the railway building bonanza in the mid 1800s. The railway companies opened the door to cheap mass transport previously impossible. Canal transport, stage coaches and a fair proportion of coastal shipping services would be the ultimate losers. Increasing numbers of factory workers could now manage to take an annual seaside holiday, or some day trips and the term 'tripper' had been coined.

The Victorians greatly favoured seaside visits where all manner of amusements, activities and pastimes were contrived for their attention. Bathing machines, pleasure boating, promenading, piers and paddle steamer excursions all featured prominently. A new non manufacturing industry had been born – tourism for all.

This book also takes a look at how the medieval harbours evolved in Sussex, the effects of storm damage and coastal erosion, development of later harbours and how coal handling left the beaches to become a sophisticated, twenty four hour a day highly mechanised operation. Other local beach handled cargoes, ship and boat construction are also examined along with some history of the ships, shipping companies and coal merchants over the last two centuries. Additionally, failed harbour schemes, modern marinas that were built and the other old beach 'trade' of smuggling are included, with some noteworthy land mark towers along the way. The images date from the early 1800s to 2010 and are arranged as is if the reader is making a journey from east to west along the length of the Sussex coast. Finally, some appendicies show the importance of wooden ship building, ship owning and worldwide trade to Sussex in the latter stages of the 19th century.

Local Map No.1
Rye Bay
(1) Possible site of 'Old Winchelsea', abandoned in 1288 after coastal erosion and inundation. No maps of the period are believed to be extant.
(2) Present hill top location of Winchelsea

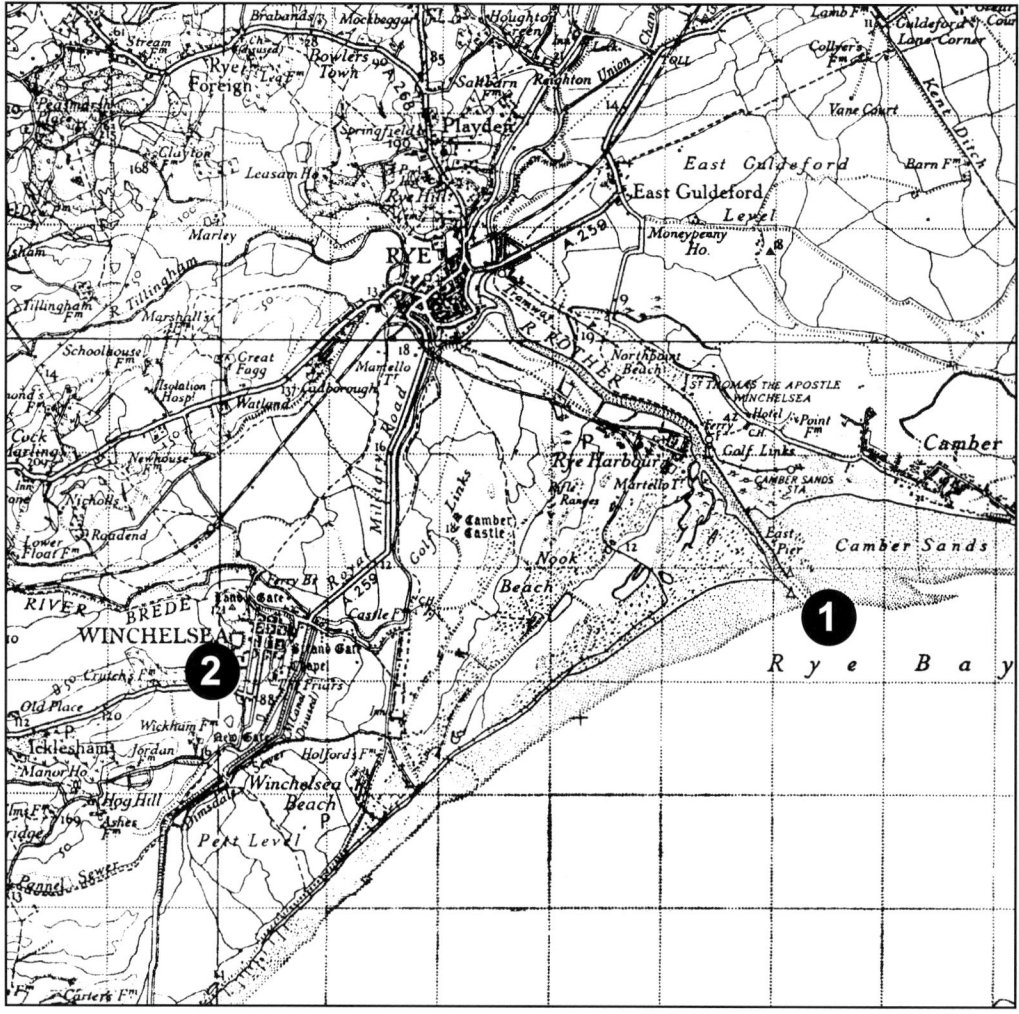

1. Medieval Harbours

In Medieval times, Winchelsea, Seaford, Shoreham and Chichester were regarded as the Sussex harbours. 'Old' Winchelsea had been overwhelmed by storms in 1287 becoming abandoned altogether in 1288. The 'new' Winchelsea perched atop a slightly inland hill overlooking the River Brede could never completely uphold its maritime past, so trade inevitably passed to nearby Rye, itself for ever struggling with shifting silting river channels to the sea. Old Winchelsea is thought to have been situated well to seaward of Rye Harbour village. The entire land mass between Rye, Tenterden and Romney has seen immense change as deeply winding creeks silted inland beyond Wittersham and the Isle of Oxney. Today, Rye town is some two and a half miles from the sea, where it sits overlooking the confluence of the Rivers Rother, Tillingham and Brede. Early attempts to cut new channels from Rye to the sea were often undone by storm and shingle drift in very short order. Only in the 19th century were attempts at stabilisation finally successful although river silt and littoral drift will for ever need to be addressed. Rye Harbour still sees some commercial shipping at its wharf just about half a mile from the sea.

The Cinque Ports

The original five were, from west to east - Hastings, Romney, Hythe, Dover and Sandwich (the last four being in Kent). Lesser 'limb' ports were later added and the most westerly of these in Sussex was Seaford. The Romans had a defensive system along these shores led by the Count of the Saxon Shore. Following the 1066 invasion, William the Conqueror appointed a Lord Warden of the Cinque Ports. In the 13th century the ports could muster no less than fifty seven ships to defend the Realm (largely against the French). This number was prescribed by Henry III in 1229.

Ships' crews had to serve the King at their own expense for fifteen days per year, in recognition of which certain privileges were granted such as Baron titles, freemen, and toll free trading rights. The last major escapade for the enlarged group of Cinque Ports was against the Spanish Armada in 1588 by which time harbour siltation problems were seriously affecting activity. Today there remains an Honorary Lord Warden of the Cinque Ports who undertakes ceremonial duties, and all the places once involved remain proud of their ancient tradition.

Hastings

Sacked by the Danes in 1011, the place was said to be 'washing away'. At the time of the Norman Conquest in 1066 it still had a small navigable creek but this would duly be blocked off by the end of the 12th century. The remaining small sheltered inlet would be rendered useless by the mid 1500s. Always exposed to Channel gales an attempt was made to construct a wooden pier in Elizabethan times, but it soon failed. In 1861 a storm warning system came into use displayed from the Custom House flag pole. It consisted of -

A drum hoisted - stormy winds
A cone, point up - northerly gales
A cone, point down - southerly gales
A drum with a cone in the appropriate direction - dangerous winds.

In 1866 a severe storm caused serious damage at Hastings.

Pevensey

At the time of the Roman Empire their grand fleet was said to be able to anchor close to the almost sea-washed walls of Pevensey Castle, today some one and a quarter miles inland. In 1066 the situation had not greatly altered, and yet by 1700 Pevensey Haven would be totally closed off from the sea by silting and land reclamation.

Eastbourne

By no means immune to storms from the South or South East, the nearby high land mass of Beachy Head afforded good protection from the South West to the North. This has given the place something of a fine micro climate which undoubtedly aided its development.

Seaford

Protected from easterlies by Seaford Head, the location will always be vulnerable to southerlies and south westerly gales. Serious shingle drift along this section of coast caused the River Ouse mouth at Seaford to block completely in 1539 when a new exit forged at Newhaven. The river would remain navigable for small sea-going craft upstream to Lewes, seven miles inland. Seaford had been an important port and safe anchorage pre 1539 only to lose its status and extensive wool trade at that time.

Brighton

The place is believed to have had quite some significance in Roman times when the coastline was probably around one mile further to seaward. A small creek existed where today's Old Steine and Pool Valley are situated. Brighton is very exposed to Channel gales, coastal erosion and shingle drift and trading ships could only berth on the open beach. In 1665 a considerable chunk of Brighthelmstone including houses and shops was lost to the sea. Again in November 1703 some one hundred houses and shops were taken by the sea. This storm was said to be 'a dreadful hurricane'. In 1650 Brighton's mainly fishing population stood at four thousand souls – in 1750 numbers remaining consisted of just two thousand poverty stricken folk. Brighton's fortunes began to improve around 1756 – it became fashionable and sufficient funds enabled construction of proper seawalls to begin. The town had turned the corner but would still suffer from storms as in 1807 when six trading ships were wrecked on the beach. The last major sea inundation into Pool Valley happened in 1850, and more ship wrecks were recorded all along the Sussex coast in June 1860.

Shoreham

A port of major significance from Roman times to the present, it has nevertheless been spasmodically interrupted by the wandering mouth of the River Adur. At one time ships could sail up the wide estuary to Bramber and Steyning. Over the centuries river siltation narrowed the estuary through the South Downs and Old Shoreham became the port. The Adur has had the most mobile sea outlet of any of the Sussex rivers, as it attempted to decant through the shingle banks to the sea. Harbour entrances ranged from Lancing to Hove, thus giving periods of great shipping activity and prosperity interspersed with spells of inactivity according to river and channel depths. Today's constrained harbour mouth at Kingston has been settled since the early 1800s.

Worthing and Bognor

These two towns are of relatively recent vintage and both have suffered from periodical storm damage and erosion. Worthing's pier had to be rebuilt in 1913 and today Bognor Pier is sadly a truncated version of its earlier grandeur.

Arundel and Littlehampton

Vessels have certainly managed to sail up the West Sussex River Arun for centuries. Similar in nature to its easterly neighbour the Adur, this river mouth also meandered about whilst attempting to reach the sea. Constrained at Littlehampton in the 1700s trade expanded and Arundel would cease to see visiting trading ships by WW1 as Littlehampton expanded.

Pagham Harbour

Until the 1873 Land Reclamation Act, Pagham could be accessed by the smaller trading ships by way of a fairly straight channel from the sea up to Sidlesham Mill, a busy place indeed.

Chichester Harbour

With miles of winding often shallow tidal creeks, a great deal of trade went on here for many centuries. The greatest tonnage was handled at Emsworth on the western flank of the harbour just over the Sussex-Hampshire boundary. This inland area is not so relevant to the beach trades described within this book.

Customs Port Designations from 1848

Port of Rye

Extended from the Kent/East Sussex border (just east of the present Camber area) towards Dungeness. To the west it ended at Beachy Head, taking in Rye, Hastings, St.Leonards, Bexhill, Pevensey and Eastbourne.

Port of Newhaven

Covered from Beachy Head, Cuckmere, Seaford, Newhaven, Lewes, to Rottingdean.

Port of Shoreham

From Rottingdean to Brighton, Hove, Shoreham, Lancing, Worthing, to Heene (West Worthing, today).

Port of Arundel

From Heene to Felpham Sluice, including Littlehampton and Arundel.

Port of Chichester

In 1852 the old Port of Chichester was abolished. Western areas joined Portsmouth. The eastern section including Arundel became the Port of Littlehampton. From Felpham Sluice, Bognor, Pagham Harbour, Selsey Peninsula and the whole of Chichester Harbour to the River Ems (Sussex/Hampshire border).

1. RX104 PALINDRA

Just around the corner from Rye Bay and sitting on the beach near Dungeness Point is the 1973 built RX104, a typical Rye built fishing boat from the late stages of clinker construction. Heavily built craft are vital for daily use on steep unyielding shores, and beyond the paraphernalia of fishermens' huts and gear can be seen patches of distinctive sea-kale thriving on the shingle. Despite being over the border in Kent this location is very relevant to one theme in this book – the eastward drift of shingle along the Sussex coast ends up here. In fact Dungeness beach has been said to grow annually by around six feet.

2. PT EARL OF WINDSOR (RX104)*

A number of small iron hulled steamers were built at Rye in the 1880s by the Rother Iron Works although this particular vessel came from a Tyneside yard in 1867. She joined the Rye fishing fleet in 1888, remaining for just three years and curiously carried the same fishing registration number as the subject of No.1. The 79grt paddle tug has been fitted with a useful derrick close to the lofty funnel and the ability to either go trawling or tow other vessels must have seemed very attractive to her local owner, Robert James Hoad.

* Fishing registration numbers are frequently re-used over the decades.

3. SARAH ELGAR →

This delightful little clinker built boat worked in the gruelling blue flint gathering trade from Rye Harbour as a boulder boat. She was owned by the Millgate family who seemingly were all in their Sunday best for this posed photograph around 1910. A small fleet of such craft would gather the boulders from the beaches adjacent to Rye Harbour entrance, perhaps just 3-4 tons per trip. The cargo would then be off loaded and consolidated near Rye Harbour's railway wharf ready for loading into a coastal trader for the journey northwards, or indeed by rail similarly. Other craft involved at the time of the photograph were the *Fame, Rose, Bromelia* and *Endeavour*. At least the trade provided an albeit meagre income when times were not so good. *Sarah Elgar's* rig consists of two headsails, a gaff mainsail and a lug mizzen.

← 4. PT CRUSADER (RX16) and Sailing Barges
Another Tyne built paddle tug dating from 1875, this vessel undertook ship towage and fishing out of Rye from 1884 to 1904 for Reeve, Vidler and Burra. In the image from around 1900 she is towing two ketches out to sea at the same time. The small craft over to the left are probably members of the boulder gathering brigade, beyond which can just be seen the consolidated pile resulting from their labours, awaiting shipment to the Potteries. The two large ketches had most likely brought coal to Rye's Strand Quay for the Gasworks or domestic use.

↙ 5. Rye Harbour railway wharf 1900s.
Dating similarly from around 1900 a coastal trading ketch, believed to be the Shoreham owned *Athole* built at Littlehampton in 1892, is working cargo alongside. The wharf's steam crane is unloading the ship to some of the South Eastern Railway Company's round-top ended wagons. Possibly the commodity was coal as just visible alongside is one of the Rother lighters, deeply laden for destinations inland. Again the boulder fleet lies nearby.

Local Map No.2
Hastings area
(1) St.Leonards Pier

6. An armed lugger of 1825
Around 1800 large and powerful sailing luggers were popular for both legal and illegal purposes. The type required large experienced crews to operate, and indeed a lack of suitable manpower in the Royal Navy or the 'smuggling' community was not a major issue, where especially in the latter calling volunteers were probably the more willing. The image is from a coloured lithograph by J.Rogers in 1825 believed made from an earlier painting and shows a substantially rigged naval lugger of some 200tons. The three masts sport large lug sails each with a similar smaller topsail. The rig is finished off with two headsails and a staysail between the fore and mainmast tops. This particular craft has six pairs of gun ports and would have made a fast and powerful adversary indeed. The smugglers version differed not a lot and the Revenue Service (Customs) also operated such types along with their more traditional cutters. A giant sailing yacht built to this rig at Hastings will be examined shortly.

7. A trading smack on Hastings beach →
This image dates from around 1836 and is from one of E.W.Cooke's fine works. It shows a heavily constructed single masted trading vessel undergoing repairs on the beach. Over to the right stands one of the many horse capstans used to haul craft up out of the sea to safety above the tide line.

8. Coal unloading at Hastings in 1854

A schooner has been carefully set aground at high water on the beach and unloading work is proceeding at a frantic pace. Single horses are bringing the empty carts down the beach before turning alongside ready to receive coal. Teams of horses await to heave the heavily laden carts back up the beach and to the merchant's yard. Highly labour intensive, all work had to be completed over the low water period, together with sufficient ballasting of the ship. This would enable a smooth departure in seaworthy condition before the weather turned. Beyond, hotels are appearing westwards along the seafront and one early bathing machine is ready for action. A white sailed tripper boat awaits both tide and patrons. This delightful image is from a John Thorpe lithograph. A full description of 'coal whipping' may be found under No.37.

9. NEW MOON (yacht 1859)

George Tutt was a renowned boat builder at Hastings in the 1850s when he produced no less than three exceptionally large yachts for Lord Willoughby D'Eresby. The third and final in the series, the *New Moon,* was launched from his Rock-a-Nore building site in 1859. At 220 tons and 129ft keel length she had a narrow 18.5ft beam and was only partially decked fore and aft. To all intents and purposes the vessel could have been categorised as a racing yacht version of the smugglers' giant lugger. The hull had copper sheathing over traditional clinker planking and the vessel is said to have required some 75 tons of iron ballast for stability. Speeds of 12.5 to 13 knots were achieved, and although the rig was simple it must have been very labour intensive due to the colossal sail size.

10. The Stade, Hastings c1870

There are a number of photographs in existence showing this fascinating scene. More often than not, the vessel unloading coal on the beach would be the locally owned *Pelican*. Built on the beach here in 1838, the 97 reg. ton collier belonged to local coal merchant W.Ginner & Son. After some forty years service in the punishing East coast coal trade *Pelican* was finally wrecked here in an 1879 storm. Built as a schooner, she would be altered to brig rig later and again to brigantine in the 1870s, when her master was Captain J.Dunk. The ship would arrive laden with coal from the north east and lie off-shore whilst awaiting high water. With immense seamanship skill she would be put aground not far from the Fishmarket to await the horses, carts and additional labour required. As soon as the tide dropped work commenced to rush the cargo ashore. Waiting horses and carts may be seen just ahead of the ship. A large heavy kedge anchor would have been dropped well astern of the ship to aid hauling off on departure, once ballasted. Several large fishing luggers, and a couple of horse capstans may be seen between the two blocks of black net sheds. *Pelican* was found to be beyond repair once towed round to Rye and she was duly broken up.

11. PS SEAGULL, Hastings Pier

We have already seen that Tyne built steam tugs made excellent trawlers. This 1877 built 107grt example moved to the South coast in 1891 by which time she ran as an excursion steamer. Then registered in the Port of Rye, the 121ft loa vessel would overnight at Newhaven Harbour. She ran for four years for the Hastings, St.Leonards and Eastbourne Steamboat Company, a brief history of which may be found between Nos 28 and 29. The ship's shallow draught proved useful for pier work, and even when operating excursions the ability to carry out towage and salvage work still occasionally came in handy.

12. SS HAWK, Hastings Harbour arm

The image dates from the construction period 1896/97 and the little steam coaster *Hawk* 189grt/1894 is unloading materials by way of a somewhat battered looking steam crane to the waiting narrow gauge steam engine and trucks. Full details of the proposed harbour layout, including the Engineer's plan, can be found towards the end of the book. The scheme ultimately failed due to unforeseen technical, local opposition and financial reasons. It seems that some roadstone and a couple of coal cargoes were unloaded here before the necessary legislative Act could be put in place - it was never needed!

13. Hastings fishing fleet c1904

A quiet day when the photographer took this image which appeared on an early postcard posted in France to another French town! The fishing lugger 204RX is evidently either newly commissioned or has just acquired an immaculate new set of sails. At around this time the registration letters of many fishing ports were switched around and simplified to avoid confusion. 'RX' for Rye differentiated first and last letters to Ramsgate which became just 'R' and would also otherwise have been 'RE'. A possible explanation for the original founding of a fishing fleet at Hastings was the availability of good fresh water from a prolific well at Rock-a-Nore.

← 14. The fishing quarter, 1913

In this pre WW1 scene, fishermen can be seen everywhere going about their daily chores. Nets, ropework and general paraphernalia lay all around and several of the larger sailing luggers, all two masted long since, await their next launching. 1914 would see the first Hastings boat fitted with a motor. The realisation by the fishermen that suddenly they could put to sea on a calm day, catch fish and smartly return to market was not slow in dawning. A lack of wind would leave an air of annoyance to say the least.

← 15. The harbour arm pre WW1 (1914)

With some of the fishing fleet becalmed off-shore this view is precisely the opposite to No.12. The steam crane and SS *Hawk* were on the distant straight section of the breakwater. The curious open, wooden piling to the inner shore end had been designed to allow the movement of beach shingle through the gap. This, had the full harbour scheme ever have been completed, would have built up against a second more easterly breakwater arm at Rock-a-Nore, by way of littoral drift.

16. The capstan horse c1909

Contrasted against the black net drying towers the horse is harnessed by chains to the outer end of the capstan's wooden bar. The hauling wire attached to the bow of a boat can be seen with about five turns on the drum, as the steadily plodding horse goes around. The operation would have been so routine that all the pipe smoking man has to do is watch out for impending snags. Another man will be leading the wire off the drum out of view left. The horse knows exactly when to lift his hooves clear. Motor winches had completely taken over the task by the 1930s. In the background are some of the tall clapper boarded net shops thought to have been in use since Elizabethan time. Three storey, 30ft high structures, they made best use of the limited ground space which would always be at a premium hereabouts.

17. Beach yachts, Hastings c1910
This delightful image shows a bumper crowd of trippers afloat, nearly afloat and hoping to achieve a trip around the bay soon. Such was the popularity of the yachts that two could easily be filled on a good day. Perhaps the only 'fly in the ointment' might be a sudden lack of wind once out at sea? The vessels present are *New Skylark*, and *New Albertine* built in 1891, 46ft keel length and of one hundred and thirty passengers capacity. Both have their lofty topmasts lowered. More general notes on tripper boats and beach sailing yachts can be found later in the book.

18. ALBERTINE c1910 →
This is an undated bow view of the larger yacht at sea under full sail off Hastings. With a large foresail, mainsail and topsail visible, she is making several knots through the water on a seemingly fairly calm day. Somehow, the impression created here is of a much larger vessel indeed.

19. A crowd onboard 1920s

Another undated scene, but judging by the apparel of those onboard it is perhaps from the early 1920s. With ranks of hotel chimney pots beyond, it is evident that the crowd will not be afloat just yet, as the craft is up on chocks. Some sixty souls can easily be counted here, which might indicate that should the full complement of one hundred and thirty be onboard, things might be a bit tight, to say the least! The vessel's over lapping 'clinker' plank hull construction is clearly visible.

← 20. PS BRIGHTON BELLE

One of P. & A. Campbell's paddle steamers is seen here approaching Hastings Pier. She regularly ran along the Sussex coast following Campbell's return to the area in 1923. The image could date from 1923 up until WW2. The 332grt paddler dated from 1900 when launched as the *Lady Evelyn*.

21. TWO BROTHERS RX80 and others

Although no longer built on Hastings beach, the majority of the fleet in this 1980 scene are still emphatically clinker built. Bright colours, never seen on fishing boats of old, are growing ever more popular. RX80 *Two Brothers*, 29ft., and RX53 *Dorothy Melinda*, 23.5ft. came from Whitstable and Newhaven boatyards, both in 1958. That year appears to have seen a final major push to replace clinker built boats like for like. In earlier years both Hastings' and Brighton's larger sailing luggers would seek the mackerel shoals as far west as Plymouth, in season. The Hastings boats certainly went North to Great Yarmouth for the herring season. More recent decades have seen the modern fleet working twenty or thirty miles away, or just out in Rye Bay. In the 1960s a typical diesel engined boat measured 30ft. by 12ft., at 12 tons.

← 22. RX58 OUR PAM & PETER
Also photographed around 1980 are the 29.3ft. RX58, built at Rye that year, and RX73 *Young Flying Fish*, Newhaven built. RX58 does indeed look very new and sports a radar scanner! The hauling chain to a powered winch may be seen laying on the shingle. Despite the arrival of radio, echo sounders and radar, and the latest navigational equipment, hull construction of these craft had altered little over the centuries.

23. The fleet on the beach in 1980
Viewed from the remains of the old breakwater towards the cliff railway, the fleet still consists of wooden hulled craft with scarcely a steel or aluminium type on show. The older 'lute' sterned craft are however becoming rarer.

24. The inshore boats in 1980
The smallest type of fishing boat used at Hastings were originally called 'punts', they had a scaled down two masted rig and were typically around 15ft. loa. In this image a group of brand new inshore types are drawn up on the beach just west of the breakwater arm. All are now motor powered and have just a simple foremast.

25. The breakwater in 2009
The stump of the old 1897 arm now fitted with railings makes a fine vantage point. The old steamer and crane seen earlier were situated along the straight section seen here to the left.

26. The 2009 fishing fleet
This scene makes an interesting comparison to No.23 and shows fewer but larger steel hulled boats on the beach, yet still interspersed with a few of the old wooden hulled types. The distant cliff top railway was out of use. Today some boats go after squid in winter and trammel netting for Dover sole in summer.

2. Ship and Boat construction

Clinker built

At Hastings in the 1820s and 30s, Thwaites and Winter were building luggers of the old, large, three masted category. By the 1850s the type seems to have lost popularity probably due to difficulties in launching and retrieving fishing gear, and the additional manpower so required. The centre mast became redundant. Some of the shipyard workers moved round to Rye to continue their skills on larger construction. James Hutchinson continued to build luggers at Hastings, and George Tutt built his large yachts. William Winter also continued at Hastings, and the Kent family produced the well known beach yachts not only for use locally, but for Eastbourne and Brighton. Fishing boat construction continued until the 1920s but with only a small number of the larger type being built up until WW2.

This note is derived from Naval Architect, James Hornell's 1936 Hastings visit.

'Keel, stem and stern posts were first put in place with overlapping clinker strakes cut, bent and fitted in position and rivetted in the absence of internal framework. This would later be inserted. The traditional beach launched boat construction consisted of elm planks, timbers and beams in oak, and a pine deck (where fitted). Spars were of Baltic fir. Boats were built entirely 'by eye' without plans, and the method of construction descended directly from the practices refined by, and improved since the early Scandinavian/Viking influence. Clinker construction is immensely strong and elm timber dries out significantly less than others – two essential criteria for rough launched beach kept craft.

Brighton and Hove both saw large luggers constructed on their beaches in the 1830s and 1840s. Messrs.T.Thwaites and J.May moved to Kingston Shipyard at Shoreham Harbour in 1838.

Worthing also saw fishing boat construction on the beach as late as the 1850s and 1860s when several vessels up to about 19 reg. tons were launched. A schooner was reportedly built at New Street, Worthing in 1861 – this may have been the 20 reg. ton yacht *Lurline*.

Trading ships- Hastings built

The last beach location in Sussex turning out the larger trading vessels up until the 1840s was Hastings. Ship building records for the town pre 1800 appear scant but it is probably safe to assume that building of the bigger types had continued here for centuries. The largest yard, Ransome & Ridley launched some twenty seven vessels during their peak production years 1811-1842. Categories would have consisted of cargo carriers, small naval warships, revenue cutters and possibly even the occasional 'specialist' smuggling craft, more about which, in due course.

	Tons	Built	Rig/Type
BEE	-	1828	Schooner
BETSY	23	1841	Sloop
COLONEL EVANS	24	1832	Cutter
GULNARE	37	1827	?
ISABEL	157	1840	Schooner
LAMBURN	-	1833	Collier brig
PELICAN	97	1838	Collier (schooner, as built)
PHOENIX	74	1838	Ketch
QUEEN VICTORIA	-	1837	Collier brig (82.5ft.)
THOMAS & WILLIAM	23	1843	Sloop
WANDERER	114	1840	Schooner (62ft.)

Note:- This book does not examine in detail the huge overall output down the centuries of the many Sussex shipyards situated within the sheltered harbours of:-
Rye, Newhaven, Lewes, Shoreham, Littlehampton, Arundel and Bosham, etc. For those interested, there is an appendix at the back of the book showing Sussex built wooden sailing trading ships known to be extant in 1873.

Extract from Bayeux Tapestry here- graphic illustrates boat construction

27. St. Leonards-on-Sea Pier
A relative late arrival in pier terms, St. Leonards acquired this attractively designed structure in 1880. The Hastings, St .Leonards and Eastbourne Steamboat Company began serving it in 1885. Following WW2, storm and fire damage it was sadly demolished as early as 1951.

28. PS ALEXANDRA (b1863)

Built by Cairds of Greenock shipyard this steamer had already spent one long career at Newhaven. She was one of Mr. Maples' fleet of Newhaven – Dieppe packet boats, – forerunners to the London, Brighton & South Coast Railway which took over completely in 1863. PS *Alexandra* was deemed to be one of the finest ships of her day in terms of design and proportion. Of 204ft.loa and 23ft. 06in beam excluding the paddle boxes, she was powered by an oscillating two cylinder engine with separate cranks. The cylinders had a 52in. bore and 57in. stroke, and ran at 28rpm given a steam pressure of just 30psi. Horse power was quoted at 200 and the paddle wheels were 16ft. 06in. diameter. After twenty years cross-Channel service she went to the West Country for further service and would later be rebuilt and modernised in 1893 with a compound steam engine and new boilers. The latest design of 'feathering' paddle wheel blades were also fitted, and she returned to her old Newhaven base to operate as an excursion steamer along the East Sussex coast from 1895. Her new owners are the subject of the next note, but they obtained a further nine years service out of the ship before scrapping in 1904. Iron hulled ships certainly lasted. The image shows the ship in final form back at her old Newhaven overnight base.

The Hastings, St. Leonards and Eastbourne Steamboat Company Ltd

The firm first appeared in 1885 minus Eastbourne in the title, when a group of enterprising East Sussex business men decided to enter the expanding tripper excursion market. There would be some three variations of Company name during its twenty three year lifespan and no less than sixteen assorted steamers operated, some very briefly. This included three small steam launches and one larger screw powered vessel, *Lady Brassey* of 1888. Newhaven Harbour generally served as operating base and bad weather refuge.

29. PS CYNTHIA (b1892)

The famous old London tug company of William Watkins had long been engaged in Thames and long distance ship towage. One of their activities was known as 'seeking' in the English Channel. This practice involve finding weather worn sailing ships homeward bound from very long voyages, with tired Masters and crews. Often willing to accept towage through the busy Channel to the docks, the ships could then give a predictable 'eta' to their owners and cargo receivers. The *Cynthia* amounted to a new venture for the Company into the excursion trade. They had previously tried to employ a steam tug but found this unsatisfactory due to most piers having insufficient depth of water to accept a tug's draught. The *Cynthia* 225 tons, had dimensions of 153.4ft. and 21.4ft. (35.4ft. over the paddle boxes), with a useful shallow draught of just under 7ft. She would be the Hastings Company's final ship, running from 1905 to1907 when sold for further service to Northern Ireland as a tender. The photograph is believed to date from the ship's latter years around 1930.

30. PS DUCHESS OF YORK

The inclusion here of this vessel may appear rather odd, as it is highly unlikely that she ever went near the East Sussex coast piers, but all will become clear. The image illustrates just how cross-Channel ferries have progressed over the last one hundred years or so. The London, Brighton & South Coast Railway and the South Eastern Railway both served the Hastings, St.Leonards and Bexhill areas, and no doubt would have offered cheap fares and good rail connections to Newhaven for Dieppe, and Folkestone for Bolougne respectively, to entice the day trippers. This fine image shows the 996grt; 1895 built *Duchess of York* manoeuvring in Folkestone Harbour around 1900. She makes an interesting comparison to the more lightly constructed excursion paddle steamers of the day. The ship was built by R.H.Green on the Thames, and would become rapidly outmoded by screw driven vessels in just a few years. In fact she worked on the route for just nine years. One of the SER's small cargo steamers can be seen at the inner berth and beyond the large warehouse building tall sailing ship masts can be made out in the inner basin. Sadly today this scene is largely one of abandonment, since all of Folkestone Harbour's traffic has moved a few miles inland to the Channel Tunnel Terminal. A local preservation group is endeavouring to save the Harbour Station and single rail line link up to the main line.

Local Map No.3
Pevensey to Eastbourne
(1) Modern site of Sovereign Harbour
(2) Pevensey Castle
(3) Pevensey Haven outlet

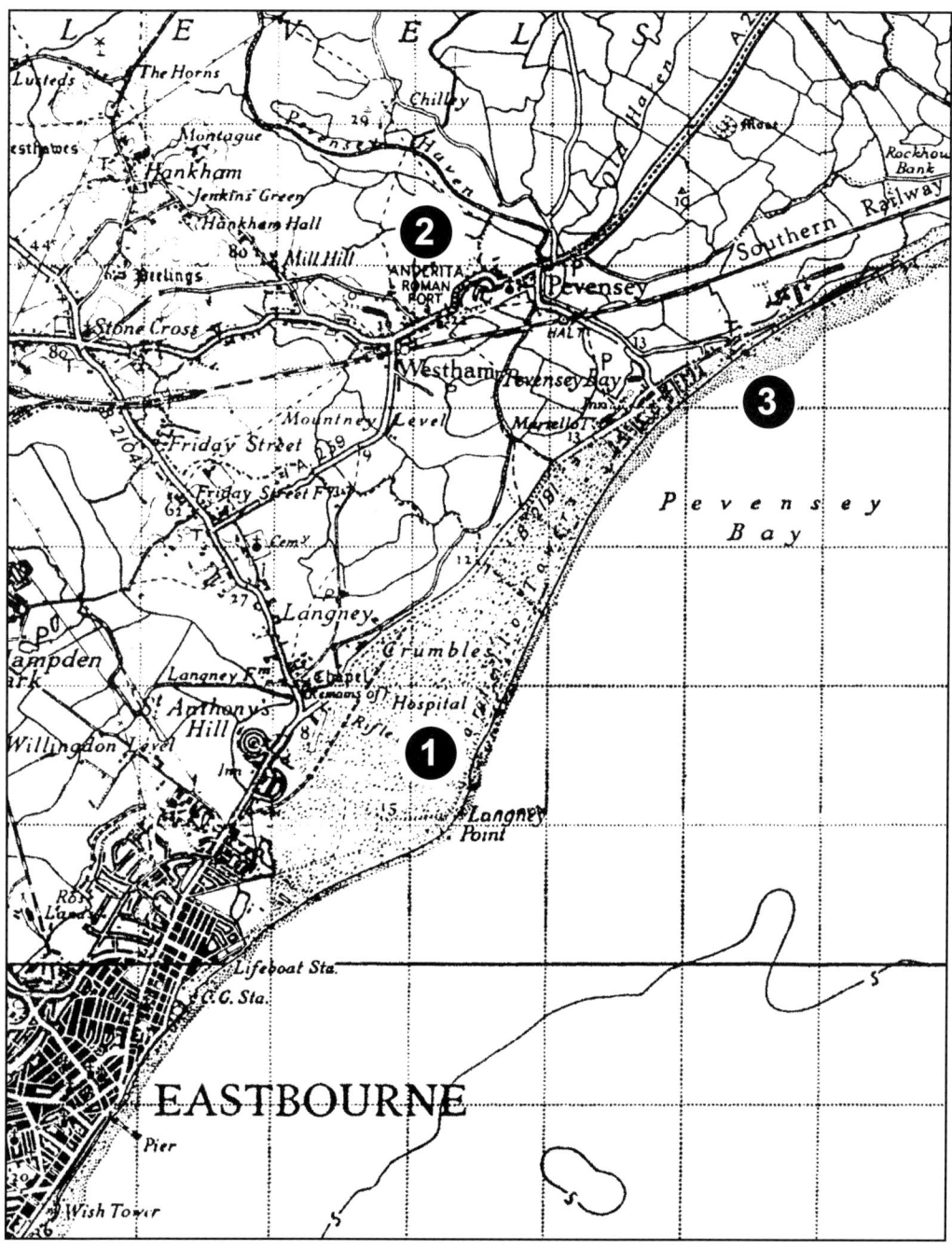

31. ROYAL SOVEREIGN LIGHT VESSEL (1920s)
The rocky outcrops of the Royal Sovereign shoals lie some six to seven miles east of Beachy Head and south east of Eastbourne. They represented a serious hazard to navigation in earlier times as just 10-12ft. of water may be present above them at low water. With modern navigation systems and today's Traffic Separation Scheme in the Channel, larger vessels are kept well away. The photograph shows an early Trinity House light vessel type on station. A later type may be seen in the book's last image.

32. ROYAL SOVEREIGN LIGHT TOWER (1971)
Built on the foreshore just east of Newhaven Harbour entrance in 1970 the tower to replace No.31 would consist of a stout concrete base with a square accommodation module and light tower above. Once construction ashore completed, the two elements were floated out to the station to be united and settled into position. In the photograph the module is being readied for jacking up to its operating level on the massive central concrete stem base. The flat roof of the accommodation module serves as the helicopter landing platform and the 'H' is already painted on the deck. In subsequent years all Trinity House offshore lights have been fully automated and controlled from their Harwich base, leaving regular visits by 'flying' maintenance technicians as the only human visitors.

33. WILLIAM ALLCHORN at Sovereign Harbour, Eastbourne

A fuller description appears under 'modern marinas' later. In this 2009 photograph the yacht berths appear well used and the accommodation blocks, worthy of a major city, well occupied, light and airy. The small dark hulled motor launch takes visitors on a trip around the development. The larger white vessel, the *William Allchorn* as we shall soon see, has found a new sheltered base from which to operate. Somehow 'www' seems to sit uneasily on the side of a sixty year old wooden hulled pleasure craft.

← 34. Sovereign Harbour in 2009

Moving along from the main inner basin there can be no doubt that the development has been done quite sympathetically. Graceful swing footbridges lead pedestrians over the interconnected basins, and residents all have fine waterfront views with motor cars and roads largely kept out of sight to the rear of buildings.

Local Map No.4
Eastbourne to Birling Gap
(1) Holywell Quarry site
(2) Beachy Head Lighthouse
(3) Belle Tout old lighthouse

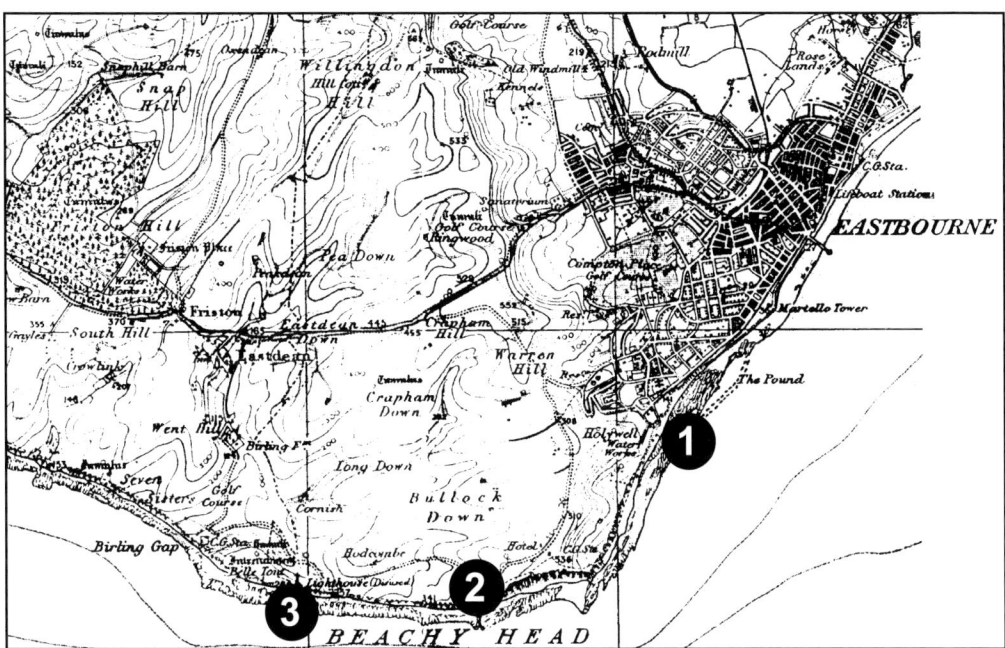

← 35. Sovereign Harbour entrance channel

A view at low water shows the entrance channel curving round from the sea and marked by buoys up to the distant twin large entrance locks to the marina. The RNLI lifeboat sits on its regular mooring. Behind the camera one of the remaining Napoleonic towers now guards the entrance where once the continuous shingle of the Crumbles and Langney Point dominated. Sovereign Harbour opened in 1993 and is still evolving.

36. Eastbourne fishing beach 2009
With the opening of the nearby Sovereign Harbour just to the east, a number of fishing boats moved to a new base. Here, a remaining few Newhaven registered boats still put to sea between the groynes. Long gone are horse capstans or even powered winches. A fully moveable modern bulldozer makes an ideal alternative for providing the necessary 'oomph' to heave boats up the beach out of the water. Ever hopeful gulls bask in the late October sunshine and Eastbourne Pier stands proudly distant.

37. Brig and 'coal whippers' c1820
Coal whipping: pre-mechanised unloading of colliers

One of E.W.Cooke's splendid drawings is included here to illustrate and aid description of this ancient practice. Although the brig shown is somewhat larger than the Sussex beach collier types, the principle remained the same with local variations. A team of four or five 'jumpers' or 'coal whippers' generally provided the power to lift the cargo from the depths of the ship's hold.

One or two teams of shovellers would rapidly fill a large tub or strong wicker basket with coal, to which a single rope was attached leading to a single block rigged overhead on a temporary spar especially for the purpose. The hauling part of the rope ended in four or five tails known as the 'bell ropes' for each man to grasp. A temporary wooden plank type scaffold structure would have been built alongside the hatchway for the team to climb atop ready to jump down to deck level. On a signal of 'full tub' from below, the gang would take the strain and begin to raise the weighty load out of the hold. The Mate would give the signal and the men jumped as one down to deck level. The sudden momentum lifted the tub clear of the hatch and in a well timed move the Mate dexterously swung the tub out over the ship's side whilst tipping the contents down a shute to waiting horses and carts on the beach, or a lighter if afloat, as was the case in the Thames illustration. Something in the order of 85 tons could be discharged in a day but there would of course be much variation due to gang size available. By the 1870s such techniques were being replaced by steam cranes on proper harbour wharf facilities which grew ever more efficient to cope with the expanding coal trade.

3. Beach sailing yachts and tripper boats

Perhaps it was centuries of launching and recovering their fishing boats that encouraged the boatmen to venture into the tripper market. Trips could be affordable, albeit totally weather and tide dependent, and no doubt appealed to those of a more adventurous spirit. Others traipsed to the end of piers, paid rather more and went for a paddle steamer excursion around the bay. This made for a rather more predictable trip. Hastings boat builders turned out the largest beach yachts between 1865 and 1890 and all were clinker built, gaff rigged yawl types of open design. Keels ranged from 42ft. to 48ft. in length:

1865 ALBERTINE (1) 42ft.
1875 SKYLARK 44ft. (for Brighton owners)
1885 ALBERTINE (2) -
1891 NEW ALBERTINE 46ft. (130 passengers)
  - NEW SKYLARK -
1890 BRITANNIA 48ft. (for Eastbourne owners)

Later at Hastings, smaller motor fishing boats continued the tradition in the summer months. In 1947 a new small *Skylark* ran twenty minute trips from the beach towards Fairlight and back for Adults 2/-, Children 1/- fare until 1956. The thirty foot *Wendy Anne* built in 1948 and RX31 *Rosemary Ann*, were similarly employed.

At Eastbourne, William Allchorn established his tripper boat business as early as 1860, and this would continue as a family run concern until 1994. At one point the Allchorn fleet consisted of:-

BRITANNIA   Sailing yacht
ENCHANTRESS (1)   (Motor boat sadly lost at Dunkirk)
ENCHANTRESS (2)   Motor boat post WW2
EASTBOURNE BELLE
GOLDEN CITY   (Ex. Eastbourne lifeboat RNLI JAMES STEPHENS)
ALACRITY   Speedboat

WILLIAM ALLCHORN   29grt.b1950 Twin diesel, 100 passengers, built by E.Cantell
                      & Son, Newhaven. Double diagonal, larch on mahogany on oak frames.
SOUTHERN QUEEN   22grt.b1950 Twin diesels, 72 passengers, built at E'bourne,
                      Clinker built elm on oak frames.

General notes:
In the 19th century beach tripper boats did not always have quite such a good reputation, were sometimes overladen and totally unregulated in the modern sense. Loss of life by capsize and drowning was not unknown. Stemming from the tragic loss of the *Mary Eliza* off Worthing in 1858 when thirteen souls perished, town councils eventually regulated the trade by restricting passenger numbers and licensing the boatmen.

In the 1930s as internal combustion engines improved, the public acquired the taste for ever increasing speed both afloat and ashore. Speed boats, often based at the pier ends where they could be launched from davits, became popular. With post WW2 car ownership mushrooming plus the advent of cheap overseas holidays by air, even the speedboats began to lose their appeal. Today many people own a fast boat of their own, which may be marina based, or brought along behind the family car for the day from far inland.

As late as the 1970s at least six '*Skylarks*' were still operating around the coasts of England. There are of course also many local sailing and rowing clubs to be found but in general tourists today, who still flock to the beaches in sunny weather, seem content not to be water borne. For West Sussex tripper craft see the individual photograph captions.

38. BRITANNIA at Eastbourne c1907

In this fine scene Eastbourne beach is thronged with trippers and there are various small rowing and sailing craft awaiting their pleasure. The star attraction is the beach yacht *Britannia* b1890 at Hastings, and she has a good crowd onboard ready for departure around the bay. Close examination reveals a stout hawser leading tightly astern to a kedge anchor for aiding haul-off to deeper water. Full use of the sails would be made immediately afloat, and a dead calm once underway must have been dreaded. Presumably a couple of well oared boats could be mustered for a tow home, if so required.

← 39. ENCHANTRESS (2)
With hauling wire attached to the bow, the second craft of the name is coming ashore at the end of the day's excursions. The stout construction required for beach operated craft is clearly visible here.

← 40. The Yellow Funnel Line (1950s)
Seen here in original form on an advertising postcard, the flagship of the fleet is setting off on another summer's day cruise. Beyond, lies the high land towards Beachy Head and this photograph serves to highlight another imminent topic -Holywell Quarry. It lies directly behind the *William Allchorn's* funnel.

41. SOUTHERN QUEEN and Eastbourne Pier 1950s
The running mate for *William Allchorn* is seen here drawn up on the beach at the operating base close westward of Eastbourne Pier. Some of the walkway gang planks can be seen and at the end of the pier, a set of speed boat launching davits are bereft of their occupant.

← 42. The boats at rest in the 1960s.
It is just about high tide and barely enough beach remains to keep the two crafts' bottoms dry. The boats have evidently been modernised and both sport funnels of streamlined appearance. A powered winch stands between the two vessels and the firm's ticket office is on the right.

← 43. A modern hauling winch
A very far cry from the horse capstan of earlier times – a powerful winch with wire storage drum and end warping barrel would make short work of hauling boats out of the sea and above high tide line. As seen in No.36, caterpillar tracked vehicles have become commonplace for this job today. Also compare to No.16 from 1909.

44. Any more for the lighthouse?
The sea is blue and a breeze rustles the flags on the *William Allchorn* as she prepares to take a modest number of trippers onboard from the gangway connected pontoon. This vessel and *Southern Queen* must have completed thousands of trips round to Beachy Head lighthouse.

45. The old boathouse in 2009
A rather sad scene outside the firm's old maintenance base just east at the fishing beach. Looking somewhat forlorn under canvas wraps the distinctive shape of *Southern Queen* slumbers on, hopefully awaiting better times. Her sister vessel as we have already seen now has an afloat mooring at Sovereign Harbour, nearby.

46. PS SUSSEX QUEEN

Approaching Eastbourne Pier in 1960 is a little paddle steamer that nearly made it into the preservation era. Built as *Freshwater* for the Southern Railway's Lymington to Yarmouth route she was made redundant by 1959 as the car ferries completely took over. Built in 1927 by Samuel White at Cowes, she measured in at just 264grt; on a length of 159ft and a shallow draught (for the Lymington River) of just 5ft.07in.- ideal for visiting shallow pier ends. After just one season on the East Sussex coast the ship went back westwards for a final fling as *Swanage Queen*. Sadly, the scrap man ended her career in 1961. It is interesting to observe that despite it clearly being a fine sunny day, there are few trippers onboard. In general the Public had come to regard trips on paddle steamers as just too 'old hat' by the 1960s.

BRIGHTON AND SOUTH COAST STEAMERS LTD.

Sailings by
P.S. "SUSSEX QUEEN"
from
Newhaven, EASTBOURNE & Hastings
AUGUST, 1960

Friday, July 29th, August 12th, 26th & Tuesdays 16th & 30th
Leave Newhaven 8.30. EASTBOURNE 10.45 Royal Sovereign Cruise, 2.00 for Hastings. HASTINGS 3.45 Cruise in Channel. 5.15 for Eastbourne. 6.45 Eastbourne to Newhaven.

Fridays, 5th & 19th and Tuesdays August 9th & 23rd
Leave Newhaven 8.30. EASTBOURNE 10.45 Royal Sovereign Cruise, 2.30 for 2½ Hour Channel Cruise, 5.15 for Newhaven.

Wednesdays, August 3rd, 17th & 31st
Leave Newhaven 8.15. EASTBOURNE 10.30 Day trip to BRIGHTON, leave Brighton at 4.30. Single trip Eastbourne to Newhaven 7.00.

Wednesdays, July 27th, & August 10th & 24th
Leave EASTBOURNE 2.00. Royal Sovereign Cruise. 4.30 for Brighton and Newhaven, singles only

(Weather and circumstances permitting)

FARES

Newhaven/Brighton.	Ret. 7/-	Single 3/6
Eastbourne	Ret. 7/6	Single 4/-
Via Brighton.	Ret. 11/6	Single 6/-
Eastbourne/Brighton.	Ret. 10/-	Single 7/-
Royal Sovereign Cruise.	Ret. 6/6	
2½ Hour Channel Cruise	Ret. 7/6	
Hastings	Ret. 7/6	Single 4/-
Do. with Channel Cruise	Ret. 9/-	
Hastings, Channel Cruise	Ret. 5/-	

GENERAL INFORMATION
NOTE.—BRING A WARM COAT

CHILDREN (under 14 years) HALF FARE when accompanied by parents. This concession does not apply to large organised parties of juveniles such as Boy Scouts, Girl Guides, etc., for whom special prices will be quoted on application to the owners.

The Proprietors will not be responsible for any accidents, injury or loss of life, or loss or damage to property of the passengers of whatever nature, while on the Proprietors' Vessels, piers, gangways or other property of the Proprietors. All advertised sailings are subject to weather and other circumstances permitting. Proprietors reserve the right to vary times and cancel sailings without notice. Every endeavour will be made to maintain the advertised time tables, but no responsibility can be accepted for any loss or delay.

Tickets are obtainable at the Entrance to the Pier.

Catering on Board. The Licensed Bar and Tea Lounge are open throughout the voyage.

PIER TOLLS. Pier Tolls are included in the fares, except at Brighton. Passengers landing at any Pier and remaining on same are not required to pay Toll, but if they leave the Pier to visit the town, they are required to pay the Pier Toll to gain re-admittance to the Pier and board the Vessel.

All enquiries should be addressed to: The General Manager, Brighton & South Coast Steamers Ltd., P.S. "SUSSEX QUEEN", NEWHAVEN.

Sussex Printers Limited, Eastbourne

4. Piers, Paddle Steamers and Promenading

More general improvements to Sussex harbours in the 1800s quickly removed the need to berth regular cross-Channel paddle steamers at the end of long exposed seaside piers. The early steam packet services shifted from Brighton to Shoreham and Littlehampton Harbours, both of which were very tidal dependent but nevertheless sheltered. Finally, upon development of Newhaven by the Railway Company regularly timed services could indeed be offered. The local piers were not totally abandoned to shipping as their steamer berthing facilities took on a new raison d'etre. The Victorians loved promenading, and if a walk along a pier could result in a paddle steamer excursion, then all the better. Great numbers took to this form of adventure and the piers displayed more and more activities and amusements to extract their hard earned cash. Whether afloat on a long distance steamer trip or simply sailing or being rowed out in the bay, there was no shortage of takers. Naturally, the tripper or tourist season mainly lasted from after Easter until the end of September to ensure some profitability for the operators. Just as today, weather could be seriously indifferent in some years.

Sussex resort piers were built and survived as follows:-

Hastings *	1872	Still in use
St.Leonards	1880	Demolished in 1951
Eastbourne *	1872	Destroyed/rebuilt 1877, still in use.
Brighton Chain Pier	1823	Destroyed 1896
" Palace "	1901	Still in use
" West * "	1866	Closed 1975, since destroyed
Worthing	1862	Destroyed/rebuilt 1913, still in use
Bognor Regis	1865	Shore end only remaining today.

* All built by the celebrated pier builder Eugenius Birch.
Nationally, very few of the remaining piers still retain their original ability to berth ships, and in Sussex, only Worthing's landing stages are intact.

Paddle steamers, companies and excursions

Paddle steamers generally predated the railways by a few decades and were certainly well placed to accept the trippers coming off the trains as soon as they appeared. A major mushrooming of services occurred in the 1880s. Early in that decade PS *Taff* was running from Ryde and Ventnor to Bognor and Brighton. PS *Carrick Castle* ran on the Hastings, Eastbourne and Brighton route before the 1885 foundation of the Hastings, St. Leonards and Eastbourne Steamboat Company. The Brighton, Worthing and South Coast Steamboat Company ran the 1893 built PS *Princess May* and PS *Brighton Queen* of 1897. These two ships were inevitably snapped up by the arrival of P. & A. Campbell brothers' Bristol based paddler company, who were most keen to enter the lucrative South Coast market. Brighton Queen was fully upgraded to Campbell's exacting standards in 1901. *Princess May* was not wanted and sold to Italy in 1902. Also in 1901 the 1899 built PS *Tantallon Castle* arrived on the scene to work the Sussex coast under Captain Lee's Sussex Steam Packet Company as *Sussex Belle*. She did not reign long and soon passed to the Colwyn Bay and Liverpool Steamship Company as *Rhos Colwyn*. Competition reached cut-throat proportions, and few of the single ship companies lasted for any length of time. Paddlers tended to change hands frequently at the season's end. In 1903 Campbells decided to move their South coast headquarters from Southampton to the Old Steine, Brighton. Newhaven became their maintenance, overnight and weather refuge port. Perhaps Campbells had met their match at Southampton, with the long established Red Funnel fleet holding sway on the Isle of Wight and Solent area excursion business. The Railway steamers also competed for trippers in that area. Another popular ship before WW1 which seems to have been photographed more than most, was PS *Worthing Belle* and she features well in the West Sussex half of this book.

Pre WW1 there were thought to be no less than forty assorted paddlers involved in the South coast excursion trades in total. In East Sussex, R.R.Collard ran from Newhaven the following- *Alleyn*, *Lady Rowena*, *May*, *Lynton*, *Plymouth Belle* and *Southampton* around the 1900-1910 period. PS *Audrey* was run by Captain Shippick. A number of paddlers were duly requisitioned for naval service as mine sweepers in both World wars. Some failed ever to return to peace time duties. They were well suited for the task due to their shallow draught and in many cases advanced years.

In 1922 a newcomer, Channel Excursion Steamers Ltd arrived on the scene in the shape of the ex Thames PS *Woolwich Belle*, renamed *Queen of the South*. In 1923 Campbells made a belated return to Sussex after WW1, and *Queen of the South* soon departed to the New Medway Steam Packet Company. Following WW2, remaining excursion paddle steamer owners found diminishing returns from ever reducing patronage. Motoring, aeroplanes and overseas holidays had won. During the 1960s Sussex became paddle steamer free for the first time in one hundred and forty years. Since the 1970s the occasional visits by the preserved PS *Waverley* and her running mate MV *Balmoral* have been, unsurprisingly, very popular indeed.

CAMPBELL'S EXCURSION STEAMERS
PLEASURE SAILINGS (DURING SUMMER MONTHS)

For
HAPPY
HEALTHY
HOLIDAYS

TRAVEL BY THE
WHITE FUNNEL
FLEET

PLEASURE SAILINGS DURING THE SUMMER MONTHS IN

The English Channel
 Eastbourne, Hastings, Brighton, Worthing, Folkestone and the Isle of Wight. Day Excursions to Boulogne from Eastbourne, Hastings and Brighton. Season commences at Whitsuntide.

The Bristol Channel
 Bristol, Clevedon, Weston-super-mare, Minehead, Lynmouth, Ilfracombe, Clovelly, Lundy Island, Swansea, Cardiff, Newport, etc.

CATERING.
The Steamers are equipped with well-appointed Dining Saloons and Lounges, where meals and refreshments are served at moderate charges.

PARTIES.
Annual Outings, Clubs, etc., are given every consideration and special reduced rates are quoted on application.

Sailing-lists and Monthly Timetables of Bristol Channel Services post free on request.

Apply **P. & A. CAMPBELL LIMITED,**
25, Old Steine, Brighton, or Head Office, Dept. A. Cumberland Basin, Bristol 8, or from Local Agents.
'Phones: Brighton 5478, Bristol 23112.

47. Old Holywell Quarry, Eastbourne c1910
Following the cessation of chalk quarrying, which had been at its peak before 1830, the abandoned quarry is seen in this image to have acquired walkways, fencing and access steps during its conversion to attractive gardens. Far left the white cliff edge is just visible.

48. The beach at Holywell in the 1900s.
Another view shows the development of the site for the benefit of the Public. A fine thatched shelter has appeared (probably essential hereabouts), beneath the quarry. The shingle beach looks to be clear of obstruction, and gives an indication of where the smacks would have come ashore to load their cargoes of chalk for Hastings and Rye.

49. Holywell beach in 2009
Although the cliff line appears not to have greatly changed in this photograph, every thing else most certainly has. Beach groynes now endeavour to slow the eastward shingle drift. They certainly would have been unwelcome in smack loading days! Lush vegetation now prevails around the Gardens as opposed to the barren scene before.

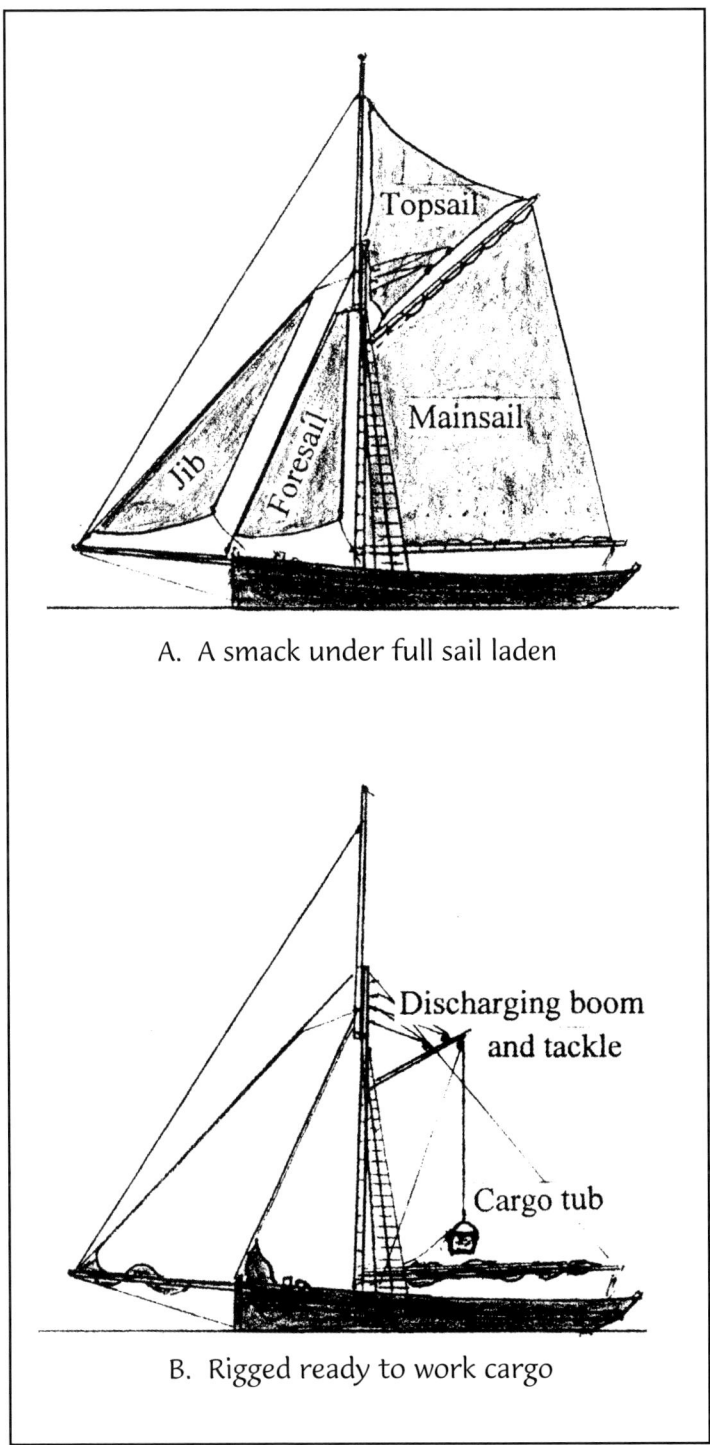

A. A smack under full sail laden

B. Rigged ready to work cargo

50. A trading vessel at Cow Gap, 1800s.
This image is attributed to W.S.Howitt and dates from the early 1800s. It shows a heavily built trading smack sitting aground at low water on the beach at Cow Gap, close to Holywell. One two-horse cart is alongside the vessel and may well be loading quarried chalk since no attempt has been made to turn the cart empty, for the journey back up the beach. A second team waits patiently to move alongside the ship. An account of the local 'chalk for lime-burning trade' follows shortly.

5. Beach handled cargoes- non coal

Much of the Sussex forests had been cut down to fuel the iron industry of the Weald, which was flourishing in the 1300s from Horsham in the west right through East Sussex to the Kent border. The trees had been utilised for the making of charcoal. In the 15th and 16th centuries the iron industry and associated activities employed many of the county's inland work force. At the time of the Civil War some fifty thousand were said to be involved with running twenty seven furnaces, forty two forges, and working mills. By 1553 the Government became concerned at a future lack of oak from which to build the expanding Navy, and therefore timber use in the County became restricted. Discovery of iron ore and coal closer together in the North of England ended the local industry, and East Sussex' final furnace at Ashburnham shut down around 1825.

Quantities of iron products especially military ordnance were shipped out of Pevensey Bay in the late 1600s. In general, Sussex iron exports appear to have ceased about 1813. Small barges carried the ordnance from inland down to Pevensey Haven for transhipment, and it is likely that this operation happened mostly in the wetter winter months when relatively small waterways peaked. The last cargoes of 'plank' oak were shipped away from Hastings in the 1800-1820 period. Sussex Wealden oak had been shipped out from Shoreham and Arundel in substantial quantities to the Naval building yards at Chatham, Portsmouth and Plymouth.

The London Coasting Trade-

The major seaside towns such as Hastings and Brighton were heavily involved in the London trade. Commodity markets in the Capital were ever hungry for raw materials and rural products and on the return voyages, manufactured goods would be carried. In 1728 some two hundred and ten cargoes were said to have arrived in London from the Sussex coast. In 1790 just three vessels were running from Hastings to London and by 1839 ten were involved. Hops and barrels of cured herrings also left Hastings by sea.

Fresh produce from Northern France-

Once centuries of cross-Channel animosity had been dispelled, a brisk trade evolved to a number of Sussex beach ports and harbours from Northern France. Eggs, poultry, fruit and butter were carried in fast trading smacks. A mid 1800s Custom record for Hastings recorded ships on the beach handling the following:- coal, deals (timber inwards), general goods, potatoes and stones.

The 'blue flint ' or 'boulder trade'-

As the Northern potteries developed, especially around Staffordshire, it was found that burnt and crushed flint made an excellent whitening ingredient in the production of the finest pottery. It also proved of great use in the Cheshire glass making industry. The process involved high temperature burning of the flints with coal before crushing the residue to powder. The trade from Sussex to supply the raw material for the industry began around 1720 and seems to have been well established throughout the 1800s. Small, clinker built sailing craft gathered the flints or boulders as they were also known, from the foreshore when the tide permitted. Cargoes of just a few tons at a time would be taken into Rye Harbour, Newhaven and Shoreham for consolidation into coastal ship loads. Brigs, schooners or ketches would then sail either westabout to Runcorn for the glass works, or up the east coast to Selby for canal transit to the Stoke-on-Trent area of Staffordshire. The trade from Rye moved over to rail transportation but died out on economic grounds post WW2. Vidler's ships were often involved, returning from the North with coal cargoes.

At Newhaven slightly large 'gathering' boats were used for collection and piles of flints were made by the landing stages on the east side of the harbour, which eventually filled a sailing coaster for the journey north. In 1823 some 5,400 tons were so despatched. One local stone collector, James Ashcroft, who evidently was familiar with the other old trade of 'smuggling', once ran his boat laden with boulders through Newhaven and right up the River Ouse to Glynde Reach, near Lewes, whilst attempting to avoid capture. Under the cargo lay a smuggled tub. He spent five years in the Navy for his trouble - perhaps wise heads in the Navy recognised his obvious boatwork skills!

Shoreham also witnessed this trade and some twenty small local craft were engaged in 'gathering' with cargoes often going to Runcorn for the glass bottle manufacturing process in the schooner *Empress* 93g/1856, one of the local Penney fleet.

The chalk/lime trade -

Lime was used extensively for the betterment of local soils and cultivation and Sussex had an abundance of chalk down land that could provide the raw material for the burning process to produce the lime. One such quarry opened before 1768 at Holywell, Eastbourne and although it had poor land access nevertheless a workable beach provided rudimentary facilities for trading smacks to load. Peak production years were 1800-1830s when some 3,000 'loads' per year were taken by sea to Hastings and Rye. It was reported that the greater number of Eastbourne's male population were involved in the trade with fourteen smacks working during the better seven or eight months weather each year. They carried perhaps 30-40 tons per voyage. The lime burning process would have required a similar amount of coal to be shipped inwards.

51. An 1829 wreck under Beachy Head

Just a short distance around the land from Holywell lies the great land mass of Beachy Head. This splendid line drawing by an unknown artist illustrates an all too frequent occurrence in the days of sail. Wreckage lines the shore and a naval ship is being pounded to pieces in the storm, having already lost her mizzen and topmasts. It appears that survivors are managing to reach the shore from the bow of the unknown stricken vessel. Such disasters were commonplace at the time. A temporary light was exhibited from the top at Belle Tout from 1828-1834 and Trinity House had cut some special refuge caves beneath the towering cliffs to at least afford distressed mariners some chance of rescue.

52. SS GERMANIA wrecked in 1955

This Greek flag, Hellenic Lines steamer of 1,900grt ran aground after a collision in fog out in the Channel in July 1955. The wreck became something of a tourist attraction and is seen here hull broken, and abandoned. The ship is of some interest as she was one of a large number built to a standard design under the Nazi regime in various occupied countries during WW2. She belonged to the 'Hansa' class of general cargo steamers which later successfully traded under many national flags after the War, including the UK. The wrecked ship would duly be replaced in her owners' fleet by another *Germania*, this time an ex British built and owned vessel of much the same tonnage. Other units of Hellenic Lines fleet visited Shoreham in the early 1960s when in the Black Sea timber trade.

53. Beachy Head → Lighthouse

The present lighthouse replaced Belle Tout (just to the west) and overcame difficulties experienced by mariners when mist, fog or low cloud obscured the old high light. It was constructed in 1899-1902 of some 3,660 tons of Cornish granite. Once a base had been made and an iron frame work tower placed alongside, materials could be lowered from the cliff top by aerial ropeway and steam engine. The tower is 152ft high and 50ft. diameter at its base. The light is fully automated. Beachy Head's land mass reaches 575ft above sea level.

54. Belle Tout old lighthouse c1905

Situated high on the cliff top, a temporary light had been exhibited here from 1828-1834 as pressure mounted to reduce the number of vessels coming to grief on the rocks below. The tower was erected by the MP John Fuller and came into full use in 1834. The commissioning of the new low level light just described rendered Belle Tout redundant and it passed into private ownership. When approaching its century under private ownership cliff erosion had encroached dangerously close to the tower and to save it from vanishing 'over the edge' an ingenious scheme prepared for its landward movement. The tower and house block were jacked up vertically by hydraulics to be moved some 55ft northwards on greased concrete trackways in 1999. The whole ensemble duly settled down at its new safer location, but remains able to undergo similar hydraulic powered movement in future, as the cliff erosion continues unabated. The photograph dates from around 1905 just a few years after private ownership. Perhaps the gentleman with large white beard had been the last Belle Tout lighthouse keeper? Given the gale exposed nature of this spot the assorted collection of hens were lucky not to have become airborne!

55. Belle Tout,
 2009

Walls, gates and a second storey have appeared during the 20th century as the old building lives on at its new spot. Far more of the original tower base is now visible as a result of the move back from the cliff edge. The old main access door looks to be somewhat redundant!

6. Smuggling- that other old beach 'trade'

The proximity of Kent and Sussex to the Continent and London would ensure an early start to such activity. The reason for such a varied, brisk and long running traffic, generally followed the imposition of punitive taxes by the Government of the day on certain imported and exported goods. Around 1700 it was estimated that some 150,000 bales of wool departed the South coast unofficially at night within days of sheep shearing each year. This became known as the 'owling' trade. From the 1720s inward cargoes of tea, tubs of spirits, lace and tobacco were much in vogue.

It must be remembered that poverty among the general public was rife at this time, so any small gain that could be made and 'got away with' would be most welcome. Many an official blind eye was turned to the activity of the smugglers. Duty on goods peaked around 1780 thus ensuring a similar peak in smuggling activity. Subsequently, tariffs were lowered and needless to say the activity soon diminished.

In 1791 the Cowes based Revenue cutter *Swan II* captured a new 200 ton smuggling vessel owned at Hastings. The captured craft was so robustly built and fast that she changed sides and entered the Revenue's fleet as *Greyhound*, continuing for many years to hunt down the Channel smugglers on her patrols. Pre 1800, an estimated 5,000 tons of tea and spirits were illegally landed on the South east coasts per annum. Up until 1840 it is believed that Hastings boat builders built 'dual purpose' craft to serve both legal and illegal trade. Hidden double bottoms and compartments often succeeded in outwitting the Revenue men.

Illicit trade, by its very nature needed the cover of darkness, half decent weather and the right tidal conditions so as not to be caught whilst a landing took place. Passing inland up a local river did happen, but must have carried enormous risks. There would be just too many pairs of beady eyes about. Therefore the majority of landings occurred on the remoter beaches where a cliff gap or track passed inland far from the crowd. Many of the smugglers were simply fishermen, longshoremen, farmers, other tradesmen and willing helpers all skilled in their own way. Good local knowledge, seamanship and boat handling were essential for successful operations.

Sadly, although their ingenuity knew no bounds, there was always an element of violence not too far from the surface when it came to the smuggling trade. Murders were by no means unusual. In East and West Sussex those caught were often taken to Horsham gaol where the worst offenders were hung in front of the gaol before a large crowd of onlookers. The gaol witnessed its last hanging in 1844 and closed the following year by which time serious smuggling activity had much declined. The beaches below Fairlight, at Hastings, Bexhill, and near Eastbourne were all popular landing sites for the smugglers before the local populations grew, but the remoter sites such as Bulverhythe, Pevensey, Cow Gap, Birling Gap, Crowlink and the Cuckmere River estuary were much preferred.

Further west Brighton itself had become just too conspicuous but landings were made at Hove, Copperas Gap (Portslade), Shoreham and Lancing, etc. The more sparsely populated West Sussex coast probably appeared very attractive to the smugglers with places such as Elmer Sluice, near Bognor, proving popular. It is most likely that a fair proportion of illegal goods landed in Sussex found its way to the London markets. The last major West Sussex contraband spirits capture occurred at Arundel in an 1860 seizure.

A timetable for the war on smuggling-
- 1698   A 'landguard' of riding officers was established to prevent illegal wool export.
- 1720s   Various items added to excise duty. Bonded warehouses introduced.
- 1736.   The Smuggling Act introduces various serious penalties for participants.
- 1751   More controls introduced on gin and tobacco.
- 1784   Tea import duty cut from 127% to just 12.5%
- 1809   The Preventative Waterguard created.
- 1817   The Coast blockade begins- established in stages around South east England.
- 1831.   The Coastguard Service replaces the Coast Blockade in E & W Sussex.
- 1845   Duties removed on many items.
- 1853   The Customs service re-vamped.

Local Map No.5
Cuckmere Haven to Newhaven
(1) Seaford Head

56. The River Cuckmere estuary, 1930s
With the distant land mass leading towards Seaford Head, the jumble of shingle banks through which the Cuckmere has to pass to find the sea is clearly visible. The actual constrained river course shows as a light strip just above half height on the photograph. Seaward of that point, the river's flow percolates either through or under the shingle ridges rather than over. Nevertheless over the centuries small trading ships could enter the river on spring tides and did so between 1770 and 1915. Barges could pass beneath Exceat Bridge to reach the Alfriston area where some shingle, sand, seaweed and coal were handled. A sparse local population in the area would in any case not have required large quantities of anything in particular. The *Adventure* and the *Goodwill* were reportedly trading to the Cuckmere in 1801, owned at Berwick and Alfriston locally. Trade ceased in 1915 on departure of the *Iona*. Coal requirements would have been transhipped from Newhaven. The splendid isolation of the coast at this point made it a favourite smugglers' landing ground. Across the river mouth the Coast Blockade watch house and subsequent Coastguard cottages survive as a reminder of more lawless times.

57. Cuckmere Haven in 2009
With the cottages now painted white, the river itself still struggles as ever to quit the land but this beautiful scene, unaltered for centuries, remains the most untouched on the Sussex coast.

58. Seaford Bay and beach in 2009
With the seafront road and buildings set back from the beach, it is now difficult to visualise a major river mouth and estuary at this point as was indeed the case pre 1539 when the River Ouse shifted its outlet to Newhaven. The photograph, taken from the foothill to Seaford Head shows Newhaven central distant with the long western harbour breakwater shadowed against the white cliffs towards Brighton. Before that 1539 river shift, Seaford had been an important anchorage and port of some significance to the wool trade. Just discernible centrally is the subject next described.

59. Seaford's Martello Tower

Some seventy four Martello towers were built between Folkestone and Seaford in 1806 to prepare for the Napoleonic invasion threat of the time. Seaford's tower had the honour of being the last to be built. The design was based on that seen by British forces at Martella Bay in Corsica in 1794. It had proved highly resistant, especially to seaborne attack. The basic specifications were -

Tower height   32ft.
Circumference at base   132ft.
Walls   5.5ft to 6ft thick.
Magazine in base of tower.
Two accommodation rooms for a garrison of 6-12 men (24 if required)
A 37ft. width encircling moat with access drawbridge (some had only ladders)
Armament consisted of a large swivel gun on the bomb proof roof, plus additional Howitzers. Variations occurred where local conditions dictated otherwise.
Remaining towers still have uses as residencies, tea rooms and museums; the latter being the worthy employment at Seaford.

60. ALBERTINE as a 'boulder boat'.

This Newhaven Harbour scene dates from around 1888 and the old Hastings tripper boat *Albertine* (1) has foregone her sedate occupation for the rough and tumble of flint collection from the shoreline at Newhaven. The crew seem to have turned their back on the cameraman (unusual for Victorians), and are evidently taking a breather from pitching boulders over the boat's side to the growing pile on the river bed. Once a good tonnage had been accumulated, a coasting vessel would be loaded for the journey north to the potteries. The bow of the locally owned and built brig *Sussex Maid* 182 tons, is on the left of the photograph. Her Master and owner at the time was William Bennett of Newhaven.

61. SS JAMES JOICEY

A veteran steam collier of 1863, the 695grt vessel is seen here passing through Newhaven's swing bridge around 1900, with the LB&SC.Railway workshops beyond. The ship exhibits her owners' legendary black diamond funnel insignia, which was settled upon by the combined fleet of William Cory & Son in 1896. This drew in several affiliated companies in the trade. Cory's had been heavily involved in the London coal trade since the early 1800s. Beneath the workshop shearlegs can be seen the twin funnels and a paddle box of PS *Paris* built in 1888. On the west bank of the Ouse a barquentine lies moored. Sailing ship owners were realising at about this time that their cargoes were shifting to the steamers. Once the *James Joicey* had passed through, the gang would hand crank the bridge closed – a job that would continue to be done often from 1866 until its modern replacement as late as the 1970s.

62. Brig COMMERCE → at Newhaven

This old timer came from Balley's Shipyard at Shoreham in 1862, and by 1873 was trading to the Mediterranean for Robert Gates of that port. Rigged as a 'snow', she found her way a few miles east to the Newhaven ownership of J.H.Bull and Company in the 1880s. J.H.Bull had no desire to progress to steamers, stayed loyal to the sailing ship ethic, and upon his death in 1907 the fleet was sold. *Commerce*, his first ship would also be the last to be sold off. She then saw barge service at Great Yarmouth but ended her days at Birkenhead where broken up in 1946. Sussex built ships lasted well.

63. RESULT, Newhaven Gasworks beyond

A 1930s scene at Newhaven's Railway Quay, and the three masted schooner *Result* 125g/1893 lies moored awaiting orders. Later cut down to a motor ketch she managed to competitively trade until 1967 around the English coast - an amazingly long career. The ship duly returned near to her Carrickfergus birth place in Northern Ireland and now resides at the Ulster Folk and Transport Museum.

64. PS GLEN GOWER
Looking fresh from overhaul Campbell's 578grt/1922 built paddler is ready to start the day's excursion schedule on the Sussex coast, probably Brighton-Eastbourne-Hastings, or Brighton to the Solent area. The Campbell brothers had an almost religious aversion to wheelhouses on their ships, considering that to be alert at all times Master, Officer of the Watch, Helmsman and Lookout should remain in the open, and brave the elements. Ships purchased from other owners invariably had their wheelhouses removed in short order to leave an open bridge. Note the ship has a staysail furled ready on the forestay to aid turning in tight spots should the wind direction co-operate. One seems to instantly know that all of the brasses had been polished that morning! This vessel had been built to include the engines saved from PS *Albion* of 1893, scrapped in a poor state after WW1 mine sweeping duties. Campbells were careful owners indeed.

65. SS KEYNES at sea in the 1950s

Regular weekly visits to Newhaven with gas making coal, often from Seaham Harbour, would give this 1946 built steam collier some twenty years employment. Her owners, Stephenson Clarke, had her built to a size suited to pass through Newhaven's ancient swing bridge en route to North Quay to unload. At 1,563grt and 2,230dwt, the ship's regular 2,000 ton cargoes were made redundant when gas mains from Portslade, Shoreham Harbour extended through to the East Sussex coastal towns, thereby closing local gas works. *Keynes* survived a further four years under the Swedish flag before scrapping.

66. PS CONSUL

This 1896 built paddler started service for the Devon Dock, Pier & Steamship Company of Exmouth as *Duke of Devonshire*. By 1938 she had moved to the well known Weymouth fleet of Cosens Ltd. to operate in the Bournemouth, Swanage and Solent areas. With advanced years and reducing patronage the ship was sold in 1962 to South Coast and Continental Steamers who tried their best to successfully run her on the Sussex Coast in 1963. In this summer photograph she is moored at the traditional excursion paddler base of Newhaven, and is stoking up ready for the day's work. The venture was rather marred by technical problems and indifferent weather and the old ship's steaming days soon terminated. In the photograph one of the French Railway cargo motor vessels is at the loading berth. Daily sailings with general cargo to Dieppe would be replaced after a few more years with roll-on, roll-off services.

Britain's most famous paddle steamer the

"CONSUL"

operates Regular Cruises from

EASTBOURNE

as under

"**CONSUL**" is the oldest paddle steamer in the country. She has all the attractions of these ships—gleaming engine room machinery and the seaside atmosphere, plus spacious decks and comfortable bars and lounges.

No. 1.   12th JULY to 26th JULY

SUNDAYS

Depart 10.30 a.m. Cruise towards SEAFORD viewing the lovely Sussex coastline. Back 12.30 p.m. Fares: 7/6; Children 2/6d.

Depart 2.30 p.m. Cruise round ROYAL SOVEREIGN LIGHTSHIP. Back at 4 p.m. Fares: 7/6.; Children 2/6d.

Depart 4.15 p.m. Cruise towards SEAFORD BAY. Back at 6.15 p.m. Fares: 7/6d.; Children 2/6d.

Depart 6.30 p.m. Evening Cruise to NEWHAVEN (Single trip only). Arrive 8 p.m. Fares: 3/6d.; Children 2/6d.

Passengers may return by 'bus or train. There are frequent services between Newhaven and Eastbourne.

MONDAYS and WEDNESDAYS

Depart 10.30 a.m. for HASTINGS. Arrive 12 noon, allowing 4½ hours ashore. Back 6 p.m. Fares: 8/6; Children 2/6d.

Depart 6.30 p.m. Evening Cruise to NEWHAVEN (Single trip only). Arrive 8 p.m. Fares: 3/6d.; Children 2/6d.

FRIDAYS

Depart 10.30 a.m. Round trip to HASTINGS. Have lunch in Consul's up-to-date comfortable Dining Saloon. Back at 1.30 p.m. Fares: 8/6d.; Children 2/6d.

Depart 2.30 p.m. Cruise round ROYAL SOVEREIGN LIGHTSHIP. Back at 4 p.m. Fares: 7/6d.; Children 2/6d.

Depart 4.15 p.m. for HASTINGS (not landing). Back 7 p.m. Fares: 8/6d.; Children 2/6d.

Depart 7.15 p.m. for NEWHAVEN (Single trip only). Arrive 8.45 p.m. Fares: 3/6d.; Children 2/6d.

All Sailings liable to alteration. being subject to weather, tides and/ or other conditions outside the control of the Company.

South Coast and Continental Steamers Ltd., West Quay, Newhaven

67. MV SUPERSEACAT ONE
Conventional ferries always had space to spare for day trippers and the advent of the new fast catamaran types, running at some 38kts, would give longer ashore than the conventional 20-22kt vessels. In recent years various companies have had a hand in running Newhaven-Dieppe services, with somewhat mixed fortunes. The loss of duty free and opening of the Channel Tunnel did not help. In this June 2002 photograph, the fast vessel *Superseacat One*, 4,700grt/b1997 was the incumbent on the run.

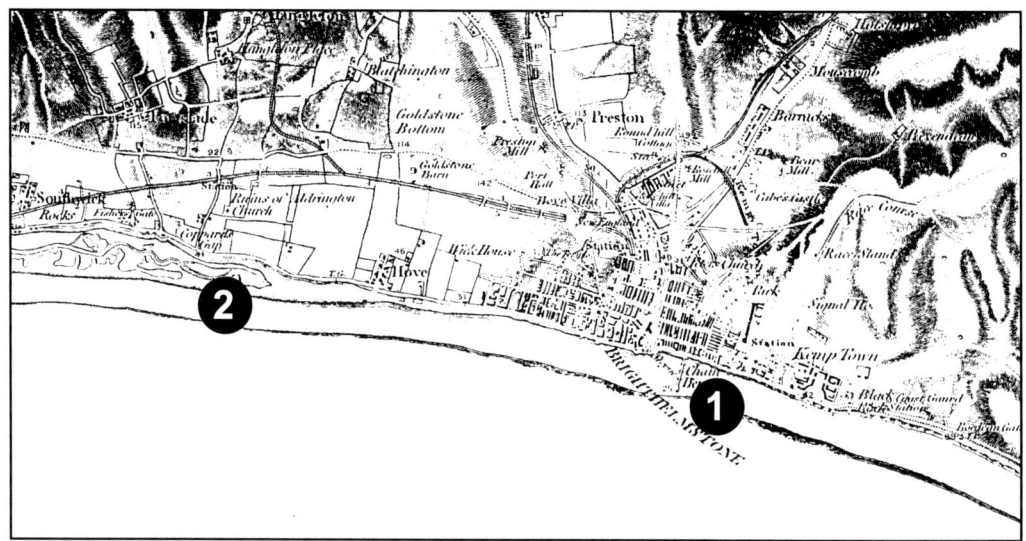

Local Map No.6
Brighthelmstone to Southwick c1830
(1) Chain Pier
(2) Old course of the River Adur before canalisation

Local Map No.7
Brighton to Southwick c1930
(1) Ultimate 1970s site for Brighton Marina
(2) Hove Lagoon, (as yet not made up)
(3) Aldrington Basin after canalisation
(4) Portslade Gas and Electricity Works on south bank.
(5) Southwick's first lock (1855).

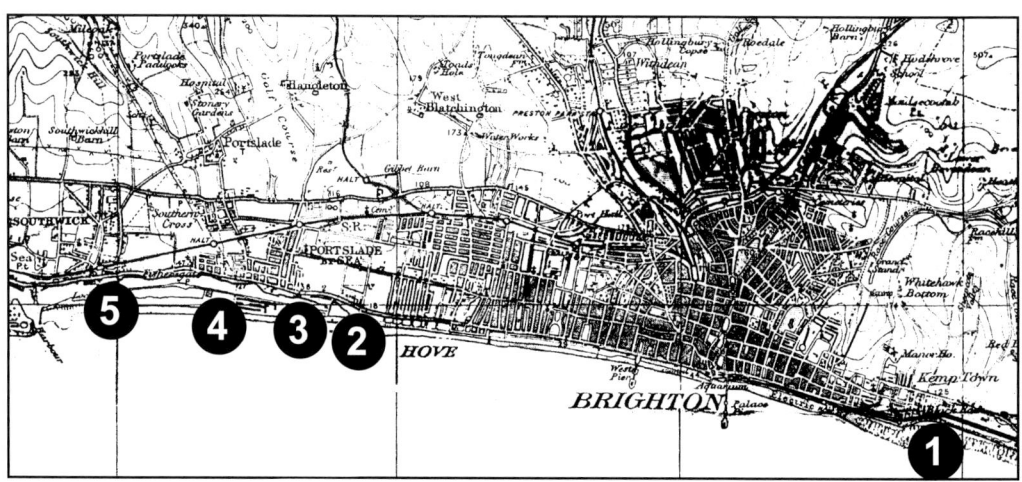

68. Rottingdean Pier c1910

Not much mentioned in the annals of pier history, this very short basic structure's main purpose would appear to have been to act as the eastern end terminal for Magnus Volk's 'Pioneer' Sea-car Railway (1896-1900). A fuller description follows shortly. The post card image dates from 1910 but may have been taken earlier. Careful observation with a magnifying glass shows the old concrete base supports for the track which ran parallel to the cliffs just off-shore towards Brighton, in this low water photograph. Even closer examination reveals a distant sailing barge put ashore adjacent to iron structures. One of these looks remarkably like the remains of the 'Pioneer' whilst the other could be that of a short pier provided below the Ovingdean Road, near to the present St. Dunstans. Both piers show on some early 1900s maps. It is therefore likely that the pier and 'Pioneer' were both being cut up for scrap at this time. Other Rottingdean points of interest are three traditional striped bathing machines and some of a more light weight portable nature nearer the water's edge. A gentleman sporting an enormous shirt collar, and his similarly proportioned collie dog are fascinated by the camera. Lengths of the old trackway base may still be seen at low water springs along the eastern part of 'Pioneer's' route.

69. Magnus Volk's Sea-going Car

Brighton born electrical engineer Magnus Volk's first electric railway (the first in Britain) was constructed along the sea front at beach top level in 1883. Now well into its second century, it delights the tourists of today just as much as the trippers of yesteryear, running between the Aquarium and Black Rock. Volk's other great project, far more ambitious, was the building of his famous 'Pioneer' Sea-car which travelled around three miles from Brighton to Rottingdean some one hundred yards off shore. In the photograph on a blustery day no later than 1900, a few hardy souls can be seen atop the saloon and surrounding lower platform. The image is unusual as it has captured the means of electrical supply to the car by way of a trolleybus/tram type electrical pick-up arm, with regularly spaced cable supporting stanchions. The trackway to Rottingdean had a necessary bend in it around the Black Rock area. One wily commentator of the day remarked that when underway - 'it looked for all the world as if a section of pier had broken away'! The 'Pioneer' opened for business following the 1896 devastation of the old 1823 Chain Pier.

70. The Car's Brighton Terminal

With Brighton's fine houses looking on, the 'Pioneer's' terminal is just visible on the left, looking rather similar in style to the car's legs. For those hot summer days canvas awnings may be rigged to protect the trippers. Seen in this image with the tide quite high, the Sea-car is making a 'leg' wave and one can but wonder what happened when old ropes, fishing nets or other water borne detritus lay across the rails? Various nicknames such as 'Daddy-long-legs' or 'Old spider legs' were quickly applied to the contrivance, and whether patrons found the motion less sea-sick provoking than a paddle steamer on a rough day, can only be guessed upon. The three mile track consisted of two double rails for the bogies to run on with a wide overall gauge of no less than 18ft. Rails were secured to concrete block bases set into the seabed some 100 yards out, parallel to the cliff line. Propulsion was by four electric motors sited up on the platform with drive to the bogies below. Serious storm damage occurred just after opening, but Mr Volk was undeterred, rendering immediate repairs. Just how long the apparatus may have lasted naturally we will never know. Brighton Council wished to build extensive beach retaining groynes across the trackway - the enterprise ceased operation in 1900. It barely lasted long enough to appear on maps.

71. The 'PIONEER' in close-up

With a flag pole on top and a ship style ensign staff at one end, the car has a set of traditional lifeboat davits (albeit rather small) to aid abandonment should it ever have arisen. Lifebuoys are placed at intervals much as per steamer practice, and the saloon itself bears a close resemblance to a paddler's after deck of the period. A reported capacity of one hundred and fifty souls applied. The Brighton terminal and building structure is clearly seen here. Given the Victorians' propensity for never venturing out without a hat, perhaps the hat vendors of Brighton relished a windy summer!

7. The arrival of the railways

The arrival of the railways, effect on road transport, coastal cargo movement, freedom of individuals, start of the 'tripper' market.

The almost sudden arrival of the local railway lines must have appeared as a serious threat to existing Sussex transport arrangements, such as they were. Sussex roads, especially through the Wealden clay areas were often impassable in the winter months although the London to Brighton route may have been reasonable. Canals and canalised rivers had also played their part locally for a century or so before rail's arrival. In East Sussex the Rivers Rother, Tillingham and Brede were navigable inland by barge as was the Ouse for no less than twenty two miles above Newhaven in the early 1800s. The Adur carried barge traffic as far as West Grinstead from Shoreham. From Littlehampton, the Arun could be navigated up to Newbridge near Wisborough Green in West Sussex, from where ultimately a connection to the Thames was made via the Wey and Arun Canal through Guildford. The Arun was also briefly connected directly to Portsmouth Harbour via Ford and Chichester Harbour, although this latter canal section survived for just twenty four years in service before closure in 1847.

Stage coaches were none too speedy as they required not infrequent changes of horse teams, and could not carry many passengers. Heavily laden goods carts would require similar stopovers along the way.

In 1835 some 5,200 tons of goods passed by road from London to Brighton, with a typical transit time of eighteen hours. 3,880 tons went by coasting vessel and given the usual tide and wind constraints, each load could take anything up to seven days in sea transit. Road wagons could manage perhaps 4-5 tons each and the small coastal traders perhaps 25-100 tons per voyage.

The railway arrived along the Sussex coast as follows:-

Brighton		1841	London, Brighton & South Coast Railway	
Shoreham	*	1845	" "	
Worthing		1845	" "	
St.Leonards		1846	"	& 1852 South Eastern Railway
Bexhill		1846	"	& 1902 " "
Newhaven	*	1847	"	
Seaford		1847	"	
Hastings		1852	"	& South Eastern Railway
Rye	*	1854	-	" "
Littlehampton	*	1863	"	
Bognor		1864	"	

* Rail connected harbour wharves.

The death knell had surely tolled for stage coaches, heavy goods wagons and small coastal cargo carriers to and from the Capital. However the opening of several rail connected wharves ensured an increase in overall sea carried tonnage, especially coal in bulk supply. Town gasworks sprang up in the early 1800s with some perhaps requiring just 100 tons per year to operate. Where possible these had been supplied pre railway by sea thence canal, and local road transport to destination. As the railways developed, inland works became supplied either directly, or from the nearest seaport by rail. The collier fleet expanded rapidly and ultimately gas generation in the County of Sussex would centre on the large plant at Portslade, with other towns being pipeline supplied. Colliers continued to bulk supply coal to Portslade until the 1970s network of national North Sea gas pipelines took over all distribution in England, enabling closure of all the local plants.

Around one hundred years after the birth of gas production, electricity generation followed a remarkably similar course of events. Local power plants from the 1900s gradually became consolidated into just a few large sea supplied coal fired power stations. In Sussex this centred again on Shoreham Harbour installations, with bulk coal arriving by steam, then motor powered colliers until the 1980s. The current new power station at Shoreham is North Sea gas fuelled, thus requiring not a single ship to sustain generation - a far cry from an entire fleet of steam colliers which used to do the job, and employ many in the process.

Apart from the pure convenience and economics of rail hauled freight (before modern road haulage), the railway companies were quick to realise the growth potential and returns to be made from the tripper market. Good local and long distance rail connections would give the Public a previously unknown freedom of movement. The mobility so unleashed is of course taken completely for granted today with all of the modern means of travel available.

72. A collier brig unloading, Brighton beach 1814

This image is reproduced by kind permission of The Royal Pavilion and Museums, Brighton and Hove. It originates from a drawing by H.Edridge although later copper engraved by George Cooke. Local fishing boats are drawn up on the beach which existed near to the Old Steine opening. A shingle bank just to the west gave a semblance of shelter. In the coloured image, a small coasting collier brig is sitting aground unloading her cargo in the time honoured manner. The coal tub would not normally be hoisted so high, and perhaps amounts to a little artistic license. Teams of horses await to keep discharge running at a fast pace and they would be well used to standing in the shallows. A couple of hauling-off hawsers can be seen leading astern and on deck there are at least a dozen workers visible, perhaps the hold shovellers were up for a breather! When this location became unsuitable for the practice to continue, a section of beach opposite, and between Ship Street and West Street was made the official landing zone. With the gentrification of Brighton and the emergence of the tripper trade, no one wanted coal carts and related activity along the seafront. In any case storms caused havoc to the ships, insurance premiums rocketed, and as we will shortly see, the coal trades moved in their local entirety to wharves at Shoreham's developing harbour by the 1860s.

73. An intended Harbour at Brighton- 1840s
This image is reproduced by kind permission of The Royal Pavilion and Museums, Brighton and Hove. It is taken from a T.Picken lithograph dating from 1843 and shows a design of harbour which, had it ever been built, would have been rather unlikely to have seen out many winter storms. The scheme was invented by William Henry Smith who was, as we shall later see, not alone in dreaming up harbour schemes for Brighton.

'VIEW OF THE INTENDED HARBOUR AT BRIGHTON ON THE RECOIL PRINCIPLE'
'The eastern Arm is connected at one end with the present Pier Head, a proposed extension of which is shown, the promenade on that side terminating with the lighthouse. The Western Arm terminates with a Fortification and Revenue Station, and may be employed for the conveyance of fish, water and provisions to and from the shore. Guaranteed cost and repairs about one tenth that of stone'*.

Notes arising-
The 'present' pier being the 1823 Chain version.

The concept of narrow vertical bottom anchored recoiling wall sections seems very odd. The routes out to the lighthouse or fortification on the west side look extremely dicey as the swell moves the sections. Presumably, the 'Recoil Principle' involved reducing the swell to provide a relative inner harbour calm.

A very wide selection of shipping is shown crammed in the harbour, from small local craft to deep sea traders, paddle steamers and even a couple of many gunned naval battleships of the day.

The proposed lighthouse looks similar to something Winstanley of Eddystone fame might have devised.

The end of the Chain Pier (left) is shown with a steamer berth but no indication as to how the pier's main open length would have been closed off to easterly swells is given.

* Costed presumably against a conventional granite block system of harbour walls.

The flimsy nature of the scheme makes an interesting comparison to the massive 1970s works undertaken during the building of Brighton Marina- see 'later Marinas'.

74. SS PRINCESS ROYAL and Chain Pier

This image is reproduced with the kind permission of The Royal Pavilion and Museums, Brighton and Hove. It originates from an A.Wallis lithograph thought to be dated around 1842. However, although the General Steam Navigation Company was running steamers from Brighton to Dieppe at the time, their ships were all paddlers. The ship in the image most certainly has no paddle boxes and therefore is a screw powered steamer. Here, some confusion arises since the artist has written the ship's name on the stern of the small rowing boat for identification. One company renowned for running early steamers around the whole of the United Kingdom coast was M.Langlands and Sons, of Glasgow. They had been founded as the Glasgow and Liverpool Steam Packet Company in 1839. For a time they traded to the Americas but would settle on UK services. The name *Princess Royal* has been much repeated over the years on many ships-

1. PS Princess Royal   687grt/1841   General Steam Nav. Co.
2. PS Princess Royal   419grt/1842   M.Langlands & Co.
3. PS Princess Royal   ?   / ?   "
4. SS Princess Royal (*)   652grt/1861   "
     (Sold 1862 as an American Civil War blockade runner)
5. SS Princess Royal   566grt/1863   M.Langlands & Co.
6. SS Princess Royal   648grt/1876   "
7. SS Princess Royal   1,986grt/1912   "

In 1918 the firm became part of the Coast Lines Group.

Given that the first ever screw powered *Princess Royal* was the 1861 built ship, the subject of the photograph (*) is most likely to be that vessel. Details of the Chain Pier head and Brighton's buildings are well shown, and three bathing machines lie on the shingle bank described in the earlier 1814 beach scene.

75. Brighton's Chain Pier (1890s)

Subject of an early postcard sent from Boulogne to Egypt in July 1907, perhaps the writer had taken one of Campbell's long distance paddler excursions from Brighton that day? The attractively designed Chain Pier was completed in just twelve months and would put Brighton well ahead for the expected growth in steamer services to the Continent and indeed for later excursions. Steamers were becoming ever more reliable as engine and boiler technology improved apace. The 1823 built pier consisted of four pairs of towers on clusters of wooden piles for support. Each tower pair was joined at the top and connected by chains from the seaward end to an anchorage point some fifty feet back in the cliff face. Toll booths to gain access were situated a few hundred yards to the west of the pier along a sea wall walkway near the Old Steine. Souvenir shops were housed in the bases of the towers and other attractions appeared as time went by. Severe storm damage occurred in 1833 and 1836 and repairs were put in hand immediately. A particularly ferocious storm in December 1896 saw a total collapse of the already weakened structure and it slid beneath the waves.

Early steamer services from Chain Pier -

In 1824 the London based General Steam Navigation Company (founded 1820) ordered three paddle steamers for the Brighton - Dieppe route, each with two 40hp engines. By 1826 four ships were running and including Le Havre as an additional destination. London to Portugal steamers also called off Brighton to pick up passengers. The Monday to Friday Dieppe service cost 30/- (£1.50) and the ships involved were - *Hylton Joliffe*, *Eclipse*, *Talbot* and *Quentin Durward*. In 1835 the GSNCo's PS *Mountaineer* was running from Shoreham to Dieppe via the Chain Pier offering a fare of £1 15s (£1.75). She sadly perished a year or two later in a gale whilst entering Shoreham Harbour. Steamers to the West Country would also call to pick up passengers off Brighton, (and Hastings).

76. A Brighton 'hog-boat' c1828

Clinker built beach launched boats around the English shores, whilst similar in construction varied somewhat in dimensions and shape to suit local operating conditions. Unlike the Hastings luggers, the Brighton boats tended to be much beamier craft, almost of a two to one ratio per length – a beam of 16ft against just 28ft in length. They also carried leeboards which was unusual for small British boats. The E.W.Cooke drawing gives an impression of the locally nick-named 'hog-boat' type. The recently opened Chain Pier is just visible in the background left.

77. A Brighton Fishing Lugger

This 1830 E.W.Cooke image shows boats at the water's edge and a large lugger at rest on the beach. Although originally three masted, the centre masts were removed by the mid 1800s to expedite net handling operations. Judging by the proximity of the boat to the horse capstan, little room would have been available for capstan bar and horse to rotate. In the mid 1700s the local fishery was said to sustain three hundred fishermen and yet one hundred years later with a burgeoning general population the same number worked about one hundred and thirty active boats. The larger luggers would go way down Channel to find and track the easterly mackerel migration. In recent years the fishermen and their boats have moved to the Marina or nearby Shoreham Harbour.

78. PS WORTHING BELLE → c1910

Once a River Clyde excursion steamer, the 193grt/1885 built paddler came to the Sussex coast in 1901, and Shoreham registry. Her area of operation encompassed the West Sussex coast from Brighton to Worthing, Littlehampton and Bognor up until WW1 when she went out to Turkey for further service on the Bosphorus. When working along the Sussex coast this ship appears to have been particularly popular with the trippers and photographed frequently by the Edwardians. The positioning of the ship's bridge abaft the funnel was a peculiar standard arrangement on many paddlers built up until the 1880s.

79. 'Any more for the Skylark!' →

A calm summer's day with a busy beach and boats just drifting about, this Brighton scene in the 1900s has but just one commodity missing - the wind! Boatmen are of necessity having to row the trippers out just to earn some money, and the beach yachts await action. Brighton's largest was the Hastings built *Skylark* of 1874 and the town's most celebrated boatman, the legendary Captain Fred Collins. Before WW1 some one hundred and forty assorted small boats worked the pleasure beach giving much seasonal employment and income to fishermen and boatmen. Another firm favourite tripper boat in 1904 was the *Favorite*.

← 80. PS RAVENSWOOD

Originally twin funnelled with the bridge abaft the funnels, this P. & A. Campbell steamer 344grt/1891 went through a major rebuild and modernisation before WW1. She emerged with one funnel and a forward bridge still of her Owners' open kind. Just before WW1 she came to the Sussex coast and would return once more upon Campbells' post WW1 service re-launch in 1923. The ship's forward saloon port holes had also been altered to the round type. In the pre WW1 photograph she is approaching Brighton's Palace Pier complete with forestay sail ready to aid turning - it would be many decades before the invention of bow thrusters for manoeuvrability. A postcard view, this one was actually sent in July 1914 when the writer commented that they had much enjoyed a review of part of the Grand Fleet of Naval Warships, a number of which had been anchored off Brighton for the Public to board and view. Of course, piers and paddle steamers would provide the necessary access to the ships. At this particular time various Naval Squadrons were displayed off several resorts- they did not disperse- two weeks later WW1 had begun.

← 81. Brighton's Palace Pier
Looking rather grand in this 1914 view, the subject last described is about to berth at the pier end landing stages.

82. Brighton's West Pier in the 1920s

West Pier could also do rather well in the 'grand' stakes as evidenced here with some ornate Hackney carriages in their allotted parking spaces. The entrance building looks particularly splendid, and steamer landing stages surround the pier's outer end. Judging by the heavy coats on show it was not a warm day, and it is still difficult to spot anyone without a hat.

83. SM5 - a more recent SKYLARK →

Perched on the beach in May 2009 just outside the Fishermens' Museum under the arches, is the ex fishing and tripper boat SM5. Shoreham registered, the old boat is unlikely to put to sea again, however the clinker built hull still amuses some younger trippers by providing a climbing frame. As for the exotic plants growing in the shingle - what would the old time shell-backs have said?

84. Brighton Marina Construction 1970s →

During the construction stages this spot saw the fabrication of gigantic cylindrical caissons to be used to form the east and west breakwater arms. The scale of the engineering project was quite colossal and makes a fascinating comparison with the seeming frailty of Brighton's 1840s 'Intended Harbour' development – see No.73. Visible over the second caisson from this end, the eastern arm is well underway. Roedean Girls School perched on high, back from the main coast road, had never seen anything like it!

← 85. Building the western breakwater
Shades of Magnus Volk's eighteen foot gauge railway - an extremely wide gauge track is here extended out as each empty circular caisson is lowered into position. The massive crane device is starting to lay the outer curved section of the arm.

← 86. The Inner Basin takes shape
Rather dazzling in the midday sun, the outer arm is having its finishing touches applied, whilst the cross arm has appeared which will duly form the Marina's inner basin area.

87. The west breakwater in 2009
The eastern end of Madeira Drive looks rather tatty and unused here, but with the tide at about half height, the extended row of caissons that form the breakwater base show clearly. The cross pier from the previous image lies behind the building. The gap between the extended eastern breakwater and end of the western arm forms the Marina's only vessel access to and from the sea.

88. A 2009 eastwards view towards Roedean

Roedean makes the only static reference point as all below has changed. From this angle it is difficult to remember that the original intention was to construct a yacht marina in the 1970s. There are now also dwellings, shops, offices, car parks and amenities as well as yacht mooring berths.

89. Marina Village view westwards in 2010

A low February sunshine view towards the distant Palace Pier illustrates just how the site has developed and infilled with construction over the last three decades or so. The entrance lock to the inner basins beneath the cliff lies just off the left bottom corner of the photograph. The outer harbour and entrance are top left.

90. West Pier's skeletal remains in 2009

Taken from just below normal high tide line, Brighton's thriving pier now just called Brighton Pier instead of Palace Pier, stands above the remnants of the West Pier. There were various periodical surges of interest in restoring the structure which came to precisely nothing since closure in 1975. Sadly, storms, corrosion and fire completed the demise. Today there are plans for a tall observation tower feature at the shore end of the old pier, and some scrap clearance has been carried out recently close to the shore. The old end skeleton frame remains as a memorial and starling roost.

Local Map No.8
River Adur Estuary - Aldrington to Shoreham and Lancing

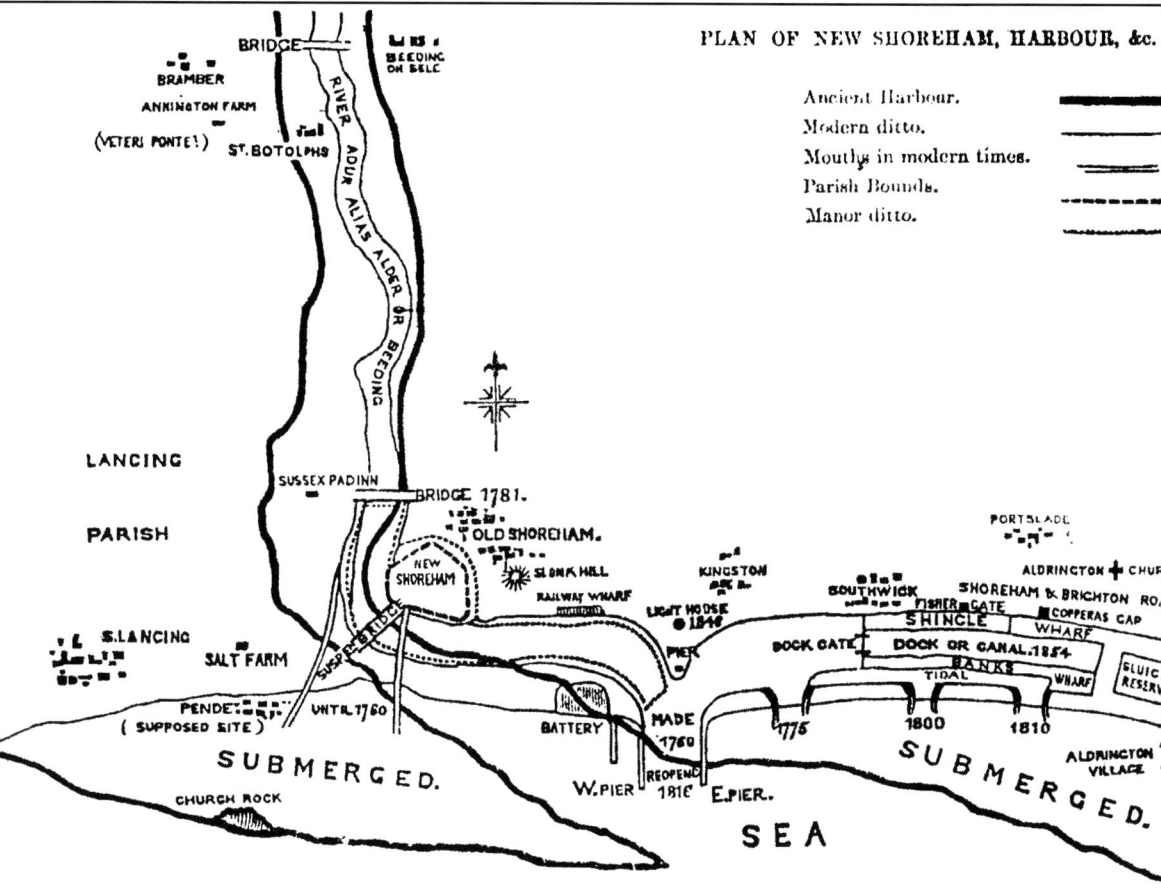

8. The long 'reign' of coal

Origins of coal by sea, tonnages involved, North-east coast exports, Sussex consumption, beaches, harbours, ships and companies involved.

An early indication of the embryonic coal trade from Newcastle dates from 1239 when a Charter in Henry III's reign authorised the Freemen of that city to dig coal in the Castle Field. The term 'sea coal' derived as a result of its despatch southwards to London and the South of England. The trade expanded steadily over the following centuries as demand constantly increased, and would do so until oil fuel usage made inroads into coal's dominance in the mid 20th century. Coal export figures from the River Tyne, and some other major centres tell the story eloquently:-

1650	345,000 tons
1775	680,000 "
1911	20,543,000 "
1939	12,359,000 "

In 1998 the last locally mined cargo of 21,544 tons sailed from the Tyne. By 2009, coal became an import here, with reportedly some 3,000,000 tons annually arriving in bulk carriers of up to 65,000dwt. (A far cry indeed from the 200-300 ton sailing brigs of old, or even the last batch of steam colliers at about 4,600dwt each).

In 1939	Blyth	shipped	6,500,000 tons		
"	Sunderland	"	5,000,000 "		
"	Goole	"	2,900,000 "		
In South Wales, Cardiff		"	1,796,000 "	in 1860
(Cardiff, Penarth and Barry)		"	8,514,000 "	1937

In the North East there were many individual loading facilities on the River Tyne in the general Newcastle area. Also involved were the harbours of Blyth, Warkworth, Sunderland, Seaham, Hartlepool, Middlesbrough (River Tees), and Goole. South Wales ports also supplied London and the South Coast but more generally, the West Country, Irish destinations and overseas exports. In the steamship era bunkering stations were established and had to be maintained worldwide, for both merchant traders and the Royal Navy to prosecute their voyages.

Northumberland and Durham coals tended to be of a bituminous nature and suitable for steam boilers and domestic use. Coal from further south exported from the Humber was better suited for gas making and allied coke production. Fine coals of less than one inch size were easier to feed into power station conveyor belt fed boilers and cement manufacturing plant. Around 1850 the mechanised unloading of coal from ships developed with the advent of steam powered cranes and grabs. In that year some three hundred and twenty steamers and eight thousand eight hundred sailing vessels were said to be in the 'home trade' – coal cargoes being the most significant part.

Coal demand grew rapidly throughout the industrial revolution and would be further accelerated in the early 1800s when city and town gasworks came on stream. London's Gas, Light and Coke Company began trading in 1812 and would be served by sea, and the fleet of collier brigs. Steam colliers evolved rapidly from around 1850. The next major leap in demand followed a century later when in the early 1900s coal fired electricity generating stations arrived on the scene, usually in or around the major conurbations.

Coal consumption in Sussex

Although national requirements grew considerably, Sussex had not been particularly reliant on coal, as the original forests had provided charcoal, brushwood and off-cuts to burn along with furze, used for lime burning and brick kiln firing.

1689-97	4,000 tons p.a.
1781	22,000 "
1788	40,000 "
1829	164,575 " *

* This last figure is interesting as it just pre dates the railway arrival, and would all have come in by sea in sailing vessels of 100-200 tons capacity, ie; perhaps a thousand ship loads. Additionally, at this time none of the Sussex harbours had seen development to any great degree. Much in line with the national scene, gas making and electricity generation arrived in the County in the early 1800s and 1900s respectively. By the 1950s the smaller local plants were being replaced by fewer, larger sea supplied installations with greater coal appetites. Yet by this time oil firing of boilers ashore and afloat was becoming commonplace, and the new nuclear power industry started to make inroads into electricity production. Apart from the multitude of land based industries that had been reliant on coal power, the railways' own requirements were not inconsiderable. On 1st January 1948 nationalisation saw 20,024 steam engines assimilated into British Railways from the pre-grouping companies. Electrification and dieselisation would see the end of the steam engines just twenty years later.

Coal fired gas production ceased in Sussex in the 1970s to be followed by electricity generation just over a decade later. North Sea gas effectively took over both functions locally by way of national pipeline and transmission systems. Domestic coal consumption continued to plummet in a similar manner to industrial. A look at coal imports involving the individual Sussex harbours follows-

Port of Rye (including Hastings and Eastbourne)

1718-1820	Coal imports rose from 439tpa to 44,521 tpa
1830	291 cargoes or 33,000 tons arrived (av. 113 tons per ship)
"	12,000 tons were received over the beach at Hastings
"	Eastbourne received 54 cargoes
1837	" " 17,600 tons (169 cargoes)
"	St.Leonards " 2,200 " (17 ")
"	Bexhill " 1,400 " (18 ")
1838	Eastbourne " - (95 ")
1860	Hastings had some 197 'groundings' to unload cargo.
1880	" " 20 * " "
	*Reduction probably mainly a reflection of coal's move to rail distribution.
1881	The total for the Port of Rye was 18,000 tons.

Port of Newhaven (including Lewes)

1822	Lewes gasworks opened.
1881	Coal imported 49,000 tons
1913	" 158,000 "

Various East Sussex gasworks were supplied and coal would be barged up to Lewes for industries such as the Phoenix Iron works.

A few coal cargoes were reportedly landed on Seaford beach in the 19th century

Small quantities also went round to the Cuckmere River by barge.
1930s   Kent coal came to the local cement works at Asham, barged from Dover.
1966   Gas works coal ceased to be brought to Newhaven once pipelines from the Portslade works had spread into East Sussex.

Port of Shoreham (Brighton to Worthing)

1828	Brighton imported	9,013	tons
"	Worthing	3,455	"
"	Shoreham	40,917	"
1830s	Worthing	4,000	tpa

1833   Brighton received 20 cargoes only (2,000 tons approx)
1859   Some twenty sailing colliers docked on Feb. 4th probably carrying around 4,000 tons in total. (They may have been held up by weeks of adverse winds)
1870   Portslade Gasworks * opened. Black Rock works at Brighton closed 1885.
       * This plant was commissioned by the Brighton, Hove & Worthing Gas Co.
1890   Portslade Gasworks required some 109,000 tons pa.
1897   The first electricity generating station was built at Portslade.
1947   Coal imports totalled 468,359 tons for gas, electricity and domestic use.
1952   Brighton 'B' Power Station opened at Southwick.
1963   Total imports of coal 1,393,488 tons which equated to:-
       65 % power generation, 24% gas production, 11% domestic/other
1990s   Coal imports largely ceased.

Port of Littlehampton (plus Arundel and Bognor)

1824   19,134 tons of shipping were handled at Littlehampton (not all coal)
1840s   Some 30,000 tpa of coal arrived through Littlehampton around half of which passed up to Arundel, or was barged onward inland to Midhurst, Petworth, and to Guildford and Godalming via the Wey and Arun Canal.
   "   Some 11,600 tons were landed on Bognor beach.
1852   Coal still being landed at Bognor
1864   The railway arrived at Bognor and probably took the coal traffic.
1880   Colliers landed 14,931 tons at Littlehampton.

Port of Chichester

1836   A mere 8% of all Chichester / Emsworth cargo was handled outside the confines of Chichester Harbour, ie; the beaches. Not all below would be coal.

West Wittering	1 inward cargo, nil outward			
Selsey	4	"		"
Sidlesham *	10	"	,	"
Bognor	15	"	, 1	"
Felpham	1	"	, 1	"

* Note - Sidlesham Mill handled grain and coal inward, flour outward.

Ships, Companies and Merchants involved in the coal trade

At Rye in the 1880s, five large ketch rigged barges were locally built to boost trades at the harbour by G.T.Smith. They were run by Vidlers and often brought coal on return journeys. The firm of W.E.Colebrooke were local coal merchants, smack and ship owners. In the 1930s coal came to the

Strand Quay at Rye Town for bunkers on the Winchelsea Road and the local gasworks just north of the main road, often brought by Thames or Medway sailing or motor barges. Rother lighters carried smaller loads well inland on the local rivers to remote wharves. Winchelsea received its last barge cargo of coal in 1930, on the River Brede.

The local coal merchant W,Ginner & Son, not only distributed coal in the Hastings area but also owned the legendary coal brig *Pelican*, which brought coal from the North East for forty one years from 1838, to the beach.

Eastbourne beach received coal opposite St. Aubyn's Road for Mr Vine of Seaside.

At Newhaven, George Robinson ran collier brigs from 1890-1903 and the ships locally owned by J.H.Bull's (Bull Line) ended their days in the coastal coal trade.

Brighton had W.Banfield, coal merchants and ship owners.

Further along at Southwick, Edward Lucas had been involved in corn and coal trading in 1822 and sold out to R.H.Penney in 1852.

G.&J.Robinson, ship owners at Littlehampton were finally just involved in the coastal coal trade.

Some fleets are now examined in more detail-

J.H.Bull's (Bull Line) of Newhaven

Established in the 1880s, and much involved in the coastal coal trade, at one time the line owned some eighteen ships. A great proponent of sail, J.H.Bull had no desire to embrace the new steam ships. Upon his death in 1907 the remaining five ships were sold. This firm had held the contract to supply the Eastbourne Gas Company.

CARBONARIA	301 tons	b.Shoreham	1867	
COMMERCE	260	" "	1862	
MERCHANT	282	" "	1869	
PENNINE	296	" "	1870	
JOHN BULL	-	-	-	

W.Banfield of Brighton

The following ships were owned in the 1880s and the firm remained as coal merchants in 1939 -

CONFLICT	227 tons	b.Whitby		1864	Brig sold Newhaven 1883		
SARAH	185 "	Shoreham		1862	"	" 1882 (see later)	
EBERNEZER	177 "	"		1860	"	" " "	

R.H.Penney & Sons (Successors to Edward Lucas of Southwick)

Robert Horne Penney's fleet became the largest and best known long distance trading fleet in Sussex. Many of the ships in the 1870s and 1880s traded to New Zealand often on charter to the Shaw Savill Line. The ships bore the names of stars in the night sky, such as *Antares*, *Arcturus* and *Auriga*, and were all barques of around 800 tons.

Considering that there are virtually no coasters left today of this diminutive size, it is all the more astonishing that such tiny vessels made a living from the old ocean trade routes, now populated by gigantic containerships. The Penney sailing ships were disposed of by the 1890s - some steamers were brought in as early as the 1870s - eg;

SS LEVERINGTON	1,053grt	b.Sunderland	1869
SS VESTA	1,001 "	"	1872

Later the firm concentrated more on coastal and Continental trade in the 1900s with up to five ships running in 1918. The smaller steamers were sold one by one, but the largest SS *Algol* 1,566grt remained until 1949. One last vessel, the SS *Algeiba* 869grt and built at Bideford in 1922, was acquired in 1946 and ran on just into the 1950s. The firm continued to operate from their Southwick premises for several more decades as shipbrokers and stevedores.

Shoreham Shipping Company (Shoreham Shipping and Coal)

This firm ran the steam collier *Seagull* 658grt/1902 for some years before WW1 but went for the option of chartering other owners' colliers to continue its coal imports.
Often ships of Atkinson's Ouse S.S. Co. such as *Yokefleet* or Rix Shipping's *Lesrix* or *Kenrix* would be employed. Later still, two of Wm.France Fenwick's coasters *Phylwood* 1,013grt/1935 and *Betswood* 1,067grt/1936 brought the cargoes to Shoreham. The former was purchased in 1939, sold to Stephenson Clarke as *Broadhurst* then sadly became a 1940 war loss. *Betswood*, similarly sold, traded on as *Ashley*. The Company's coal wharf at Southwick eventually became part of the Corrall's empire, thence part of the Powell Dufferin (P.D.Fuels) Group.

Brighton Corporation

The famous local electric railway pioneer, Magnus Volk had experimented with a steam driven dynamo to light a Royal Pavilion concert in 1881. Shortly thereafter, the Hammond Electric Light and Power Company, started to supply consumers, believed to be the first such enterprise in the United Kingdom. By 1891 the Hammond Company had become the Brighton and Hove Electric Company. A larger power station was constructed on the South Bank of Southwick Canal in 1906. The plant would be served by the growing fleet of steam colliers owned by Stephenson Clarke, in addition to their local gasworks deliveries at Portslade. In 1936, Brighton Corporation decided to build and operate two colliers of their own to serve the electricity works. *Henry Moon* 1,091grt/1936 and identical sister vessel *Arthur Wright* 1,091grt/1937, entered service with the Company's funnel logo, a stylised 'EBU' on display. This stood for 'Brighton Electricity Undertaking'. Following WW2 the power generation industry was nationalised in 1948 under the British Electricity Authority. Their expanding fleet of colliers became re-branded again in 1958 under the Central Electricity Authority.

Stephenson Clarke

Remarkably still trading in 2010, the origins of this firm go back to 1730 when Ralph and Robert Clarke purchased a schooner. In 1775, one son of Robert, John Clarke, married Jane Stephenson and their subsequent move to London saw the ship owning and coal factor business rapidly progress. The firm became part of the giant Powell Dufferin Group in 1928. Contracts to supply and deliver coal to major gas producers and later electricity generating stations became the Company's bread and butter, along with other industrial and domestic coal cargo delivery. The first SS *Shoreham* 491grt/1872 became a much repeated name over the years, and the majority of the fleet carried names of Sussex towns and villages plus several from elsewhere around the South coast area served.
In 1892 in order to acquire further coal business the Company made a surprise move by going back into sailing colliers with the purchase of four elderly brigs at Shoreham from T.P.Cattley & Co; plus one further from W.Pannett of Newhaven, previously owned by Banfields of Brighton. The brigs were kept in the fleet until around 1899 when sold for further trading-

ALICE V.GOODHUE	151g/1861	Sold J.Robinson, Littlehampton
CONFLICT	227n/1864	(lost in 1894 en route Shoreham)
EBERNEZER	177g/1860	Sold J.Robinson, Littlehampton
PROSPERO	144g/1856	b. Rye, sold to West Hartlepool
SARAH	185g/1862	b.Shoreham, sold J.Robinson, L'ton

Coastal shipping presented a hazardous occupation for those involved especially in the days of sail. Storms, collisions and groundings were not uncommon even during the steamer period when modern navigational aids had yet to appear. The two World Wars also took a terrible toll on both coastal and deep sea shipping. Listed below are names of some vessels lost in the coastal coal trade service of just one Company. It is included here simply as a tribute to those courageous coastal mariners who, at the time kept the rest of the population going with heat, light and power. The vast majority of the ships' crews were thankfully rescued.

Name	Tonnage/Year	Fate
SHOREHAM	491g/1872	Lost en route Shoreham after collision 1888
CONFLICT	(see above Disappeared 1894)	
JOHN MILES	687g/1908	Sunk by U-boat en route Shoreham 1917
PULBOROUGH	960g/1933	Sunk by air attack en route Sh'm 1940
PORTSLADE II	1,091g/1936	" " " "
BROADHURST I	1,013g/1935	Sunk by E-boat " "
AMBERLEY	1,943g/1953	Lost in heavy weather " 1973

Also, managed by the Company-
HENRY MOON   1,091g/1936   Sunk by air attack en route Shoreham 1940

After WW2 motor coasters began to replace the steamers and these continued to serve Portslade Gasworks until its closure, and also local domestic coal supplies. Following the opening at Southwick in 1957 of the much larger Prince Philip Lock, 4,000 ton ships belonging to the Company, and ships managed for the C.E.G.B. continued to bring coal to Brighton 'B' Power Station at Southwick until its demise. As the overall coastal coal trade continued to peter out, colliers were re-branded as 'mini-bulkers' to reflect their ability to carry any dry bulk cargo. Stephenson Clarke ships still visit Shoreham from time to time in the quarried aggregate trades, for example. Long may they flourish!

Robinsons of Littlehampton

In the 1870s G.&J. Robinsons' fleet of sailing vessels were well known in both deep sea and the coastal trades. Some traded as far as the East Indies, Americas and the Mediterranean, others to the Baltic Sea. By the 1890s sail was becoming largely outmoded in the international ocean trades, however some work could still be found in the coastal coal and Baltic timber trades for such ships remaining. The three brigs already described - *Alice V.Goodhue, Ebernezer* and *Sarah* were purchased for Littlehampton's coal trade in 1895/6. The old Shoreham built brig (latterly brigantine) *Ebernezer* had the honour of being the port's last sailing ship. Sold in 1915, she was sunk by a U-boat in the Channel in 1917. Coal continued to come to Littlehampton in steam and then motor coasters post WW2.

91. Kingston's 1846 built lighthouse →

Standing close by the coast road between Southwick and Shoreham is this neat little stone lighthouse standing guard over the entrance to Shoreham Harbour. This marks the point at which the meandering mouth of the River Adur finally became constrained by man in 1818. The light tower forms the upper leading light to guide ships either into the River Adur or eastwards to Southwick Locks. The photograph dates from 2010.

92. SS F.E.WEBB at Southwick, 1900s
Once Brighton's beach coal trade drew to a close, the eastern extremity of Shoreham Harbour, reached after 1855 by the canalised old river bed of the Adur, would take the trade. This was made possible by the opening of the first Southwick sea lock. Domestic coal wharves along with gasworks and power stations sprang up along the section from Aldrington to Portslade. The steam colliers could remain afloat at all times, and be serviced by high capacity steam powered grab cranes for speedy discharge. In this fine scene, Stephenson Clarke's collier *F.E.Webb* 585grt/1891 has discharged her coal cargo further along the canal and is now ready to return to the North-east coast for the next load. This ship served until 1912 when sold to other London owners. The lock shown here became the port's drydock later when larger sea locks were built. It is still in service today as the Adur Drydock. Far distant right are the buildings of the first electricity generating station opposite Fishersgate.

93. Portslade Gasworks → and mechanised coal unloading, 1900s
A pair of high level tracked steam cranes make short work here of unloading a collier. The crane driver, exposed to the elements can be seen at the controls close to the tall vertical boiler without cab protection, perhaps it kept him warm in winter! The ship is possibly SS *Portslade* of 634 grt; there being a number of similar vessels in the Stephenson Clarke fleet at the time. A Scandinavian grey hulled timber ship is moored over at the Baltic Wharf on the Portslade side of the Canal. This image makes an interesting comparison to No.37, as it illustrates the transition from manual to mechanised coal discharge.

94. PS ALEXANDRA (b1879)

A paddler with an interesting history built by Scott & Co. Greenock, this iron hulled vessel first went into the service operated jointly by the London, Brighton & South Coast Railway, with the London & South Western Railway between Portsmouth and Ryde. Her dimensions were 171ft by 20ft hull width and the engines could produce 120hp. Upon sale after thirty years service she went briefly to the Bembridge and Seaview Steam Packet Company but probably proved a bit too big for Bembridge Harbour's shallows. By 1914 she was running for the famous paddler firm of Cosens Ltd, at Weymouth. In 1933 she came to Shoreham as a 'show boat'. This did not last and in 1934 the London steam tug *Venturous* 179grt/1904 came to tow the old ship to Thomas Ward's scrapyard on the Thames. An altercation appears to have occurred between *Alexandra* and the Shoreham to Shoreham Beach concrete footbridge upon departure, the sliding section not being a very wide opening.

95. SS ALGEIBA →

A detailed item about this shipowner's history appeared in the 'coal section'. *Algeiba* 869grt/1923 would be the last vessel owned by Penney's of Southwick. This ship had been purchased in 1946 as *Runnelstone* and she would have often worked coastal coal cargoes. The rather box-like accommodation right over the poop deck was likely to have been a WW2 addition, housing radio communications and possibly gunners during those dangerous coastal convoy runs.

96. SS ELEANOR BROOKE →

In 1933 a second larger lock opened alongside the 1855 original at Southwick. This would permit a new generation of larger colliers and other vessels to visit the Canal as far as Aldrington Basin, Hove. In this 1950s image *Eleanor Brooke* 1,091grt/ 1,505dwt is arriving with coal from the North East for either the gas or electricity works. With dimensions of 225.5ft by 34.2ft and 14.7ft draught she could easily pass through the new Prince George Lock. Scores of coasters were built to very similar dimension in the 1930s and up until the 1950s and they would be able to handle cargoes of around 1,600 tons. *Eleanor Brooke* and a number of near sister vessels were made redundant after the local opening in 1957 of the new much larger Prince Philip Lock at Southwick. In the photograph the buildings and white cliffs at Brighton are visible over the ship's bow.

ALGEIBA

ELEANOR BROOKE

97. Inshore fishermen, Southwick, 1965

A small group of the last local clinker built craft lie at their moorings just outside of the old end wall of the Adur Drydock, where the 1855 lock opened to the sea. Beyond at Albion Wharf the German timber ship *Maria Nibbe* 422grt/1958 awaits discharge. Just beyond her was Penney's Oil Wharf and further still, Corrall's domestic coal wharf with its two travelling gantry cranes.

98. SS SIR JOHN SNELL →

The construction of Brighton 'B' Power Station at Southwick and its opening in 1952 became the catalyst for major harbour expansion at Shoreham to permit a new, much larger generation of colliers to visit the port. The new Prince Philip Lock could accept ships of up to around three hundred and forty feet in length with a carrying capacity of 3,700 tons, and nearer to 4,500 tons on spring tides. In the 1966 photograph, one of the regular quartet of steam colliers is partly discharged at the power station stock yard. At 2,947grt/ 3,700dwt the *Sir John Snell* served the installation until she met with the scrap man in 1980. Although very conventionally powered by steam reciprocating engines this class of vessel had oil fired boilers as built in 1955.

99. SS W.J.H.WOOD →

This vessel belonged to an earlier class of steam collier built to serve Thames side and Ipswich power stations around 1950. At 3,357grt some 4,500 tons of coal could be carried on a deeper draught of 20ft. Following the 1957 alterations at Shoreham such vessels could access the port on the fortnightly higher spring tides. These ships entered service with coal fired boilers but were later converted to oil firing by the 1960s. *W.J.H.Wood* left the Central Electricity Generating Board fleet for other owners in 1974. The very last British steam collier in service, sister vessel *Cliff Quay* finally went for scrap after bringing her last cargo of coal to Shoreham in 1983. One century earlier and the average cargo would have been in the region of 800-900 tons. In 1773 it was more likely to have been nearer to 100-200 tons per sailing collier.

100. Colliers at Brighton 'B' Power Station c1970

The scene at Southwick, little altered between 1957 and 1983, shows three large steam colliers berthed and in various stages of unloading. The nearest is SS *Arundel* 3,422grt/4,600 dwt and the last of her type to be built in 1956, for Stephenson Clarke. Astern are two of the regulars - *James Rowan* and *Sir William Walker*. Between these three some 11,500 tons of power station coal would be added to the stock yard pile.

101. MV DULWICH →

Portslade Gasworks had been largely supplied by Stephenson Clarke's fleet since its 1870 construction. In 1949 the South Eastern Gas Board had taken over a number of smaller local companies and increased their own fleet of mainly Thames up-river colliers to serve their installations. With the impending arrival of North Sea gas in the 1970s, many coal gas generating stations started to be wound down for closure. The Company's motor flat-iron colliers had diminishing employment prospects. In this photograph their MV *Dulwich* 1,873grt/1957 has brought coal to Portslade Gasworks in 1970, and would shortly be sold to Stephenson Clarke for further general trading under the name *Worthing*. The gasworks would duly part convert to gas from LPG production, and would close completely after just over one century of production.

102. MV STORRINGTON →

Although built to the familiar collier layout with a midships bridge, this Stephenson Clarke ship was fitted out with a full set of cargo derricks and winches for general worldwide trading. At 3,809grt/5,000 dwt *Storrington's* propulsion embraced motor technology fully in 1959, the year of her build. In the 1978 photograph entering Southwick Canal, the ship is flying a quarantine flag indicating this was no plain coastal voyage. The Newhaven tug *Metrec* is providing assistance at the bow and it would not be long before the ship's sale to Cypriot owners for further trading. Cargoes of coal had on occasion been brought to Shoreham by the *Storrington* in her earlier years. Between the tug and the ship's bow the harbour steam dredger *Adur* and a hopper barge lie at their customary moorings.

Local Map No.9
Worthing area
(1) Old Heene

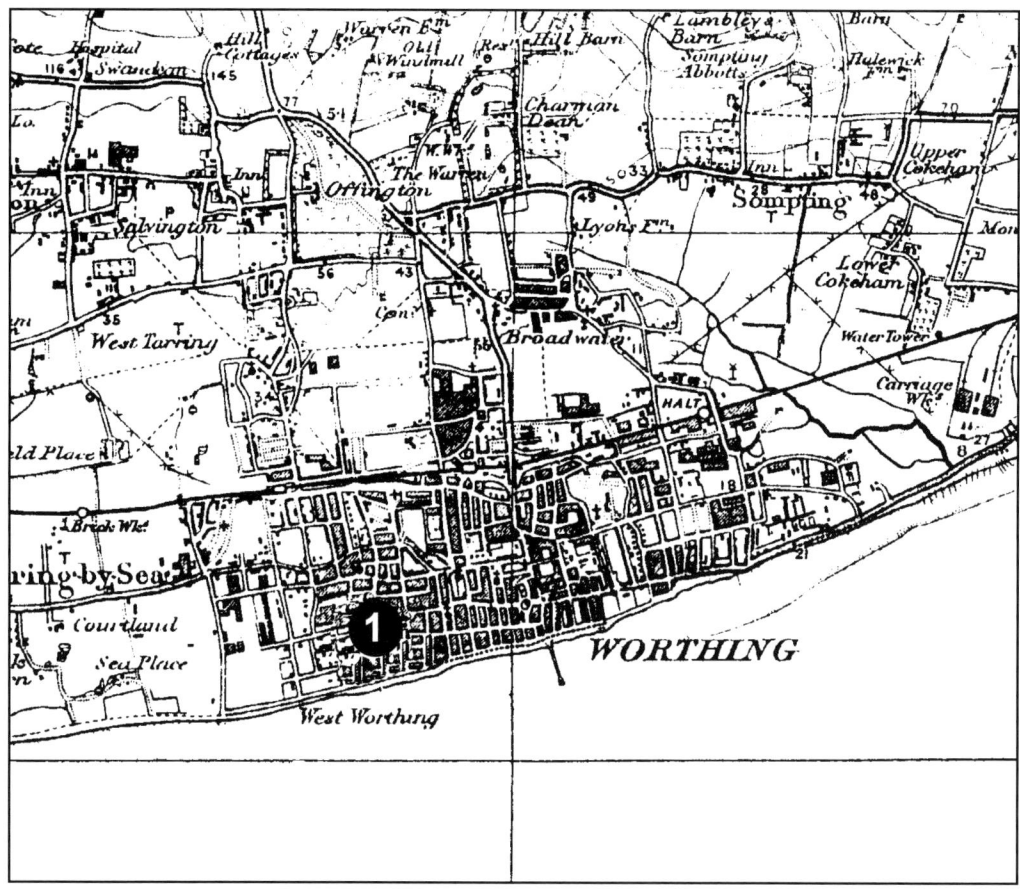

103. FOREST BELLE? At Worthing in the 1870s? ↗
There is some doubt over the identification of the ship in this unusual image. What is certain is that empty carts are being brought down the beach to receive cargo from a three masted topsail schooner. Extra horses can be seen heaving the laden carts back up the beach beyond, over the shingle ridge to the road. The vessel is thought to be the *Forest Belle* of Chester, 122 reg. tons, and owned at the time by Sloane of Chester. She traded all around the UK coasts for a couple of decades after her completion by a Newport, South Wales shipyard in 1870. She may be unloading coal and yet there is little evidence of any rigging normally so required for that pursuit. Note the heavy anchor dragged out and set in the sand to aid hauling off at departure time. It is quite possible that coal may still have come to Worthing's beach in the 1870s before its total import at Shoreham Harbour.

104. A smoky → departure from Worthing Pier c1910
A stoker is piling on the coal in the boiler furnace as *Worthing Belle* sets off, having landed all her passengers at the end of a calm day's service. This fine image is from a glass slide taken between 1901-1914, which appears to have been a grand period for excursion paddle steamers generally.

105. Worthing beach trippers

There's a good crowd in, out and on the sea in this scene from the 1950s. Two local clinker built boats are plying their summer trade from the wheeled walkway pushed out into the sea. The nearest boat, SM553 probably fishes in winter and they have found some flags to dress overall for the tripper trade. In the 1950s also, an ex WW2 Army DUKW amphibious vehicle plied trippers out from this beach. It can just be made out sitting mid picture on the shingle beach.

106. PS WAVERLEY

Once Cosens of Weymouth and British Rail's last two Portsmouth paddlers had ceased operating around 1967, there were no more paddle steamer trips on offer along the whole South coast. *Waverley* 693grt/1947, a former River Clyde vessel, had already begun her second career under the auspices of the Paddle Steamer Preservation Society from 1975. By visiting many coastal piers she could offer once again the joys of a steamer trip locally, and in this 1978 scene she is departing Worthing Pier for the Solent area at the end of a long day's steaming along the Sussex coast. The image is interesting because at the time both of the ship's funnels were still in use for their intended purpose - as boiler uptakes. Later, she would be reboilered and variously improved and rebuilt for continuing service. Note she also still carried a Decca 'cheese' type radar scanner, and still had three out of four original lifeboats. The after boats were duly replaced by racks of liferafts. Another delightful feature visible is the old style destination board to greet the boarders – Ryde, Portsmouth and Southampton displayed! Thankfully the old ship is today as good as ever after many refits, rebuilds and repaints, largely still courtesy of her army of faithfull supporters.

107. Worthing Pier in 2009
A June 2009 view and the pier is in fine order complete with end landing stages to seaward. Originally built in 1862 it had to be rebuilt after destruction in 1913. There are few working fishing boats now on Worthing's main beach, but a number still put to sea just along at East Worthing.

108. MV BALMORAL at Worthing Pier in 2009
At the end of June 2009 the running mate to *Waverley* spent some time sailing in and around the Solent area as part of her sixty year celebrations. She entered service on Red Funnel's Southampton - West Cowes route in 1949, and served there until 1968 when a move to Campbell's Bristol Channel services followed. Later, she became the running mate and fund raiser for the Paddle Steamer Preservation Society's *Waverley* project. Now very popular around the coasts with her own loyal following, she is seen here at Worthing arriving from Ryde, with a good load of traditional trippers.

109. 'Some off, and many more on'
Beneath *Balmoral's* immaculate Thorneycroft design funnel some folk from Ryde and Portsmouth have opted for an afternoon sampling the sedate delights of Worthing. An even larger number of patrons are embarking for a celebratory Sussex coast cruise towards Beachy Head.

110. A Sussex coast cruise in 2009

In this photograph the well laden ship is moving astern to clear Worthing Pier to turn eastwards. With just *Waverley* and *Balmoral's* occasional visits to the area, and so few piers able still to accept them, it is not at all surprising that the Public shows such great interest. Long may it continue!

Local Map No.10
Littlehampton to Arundel

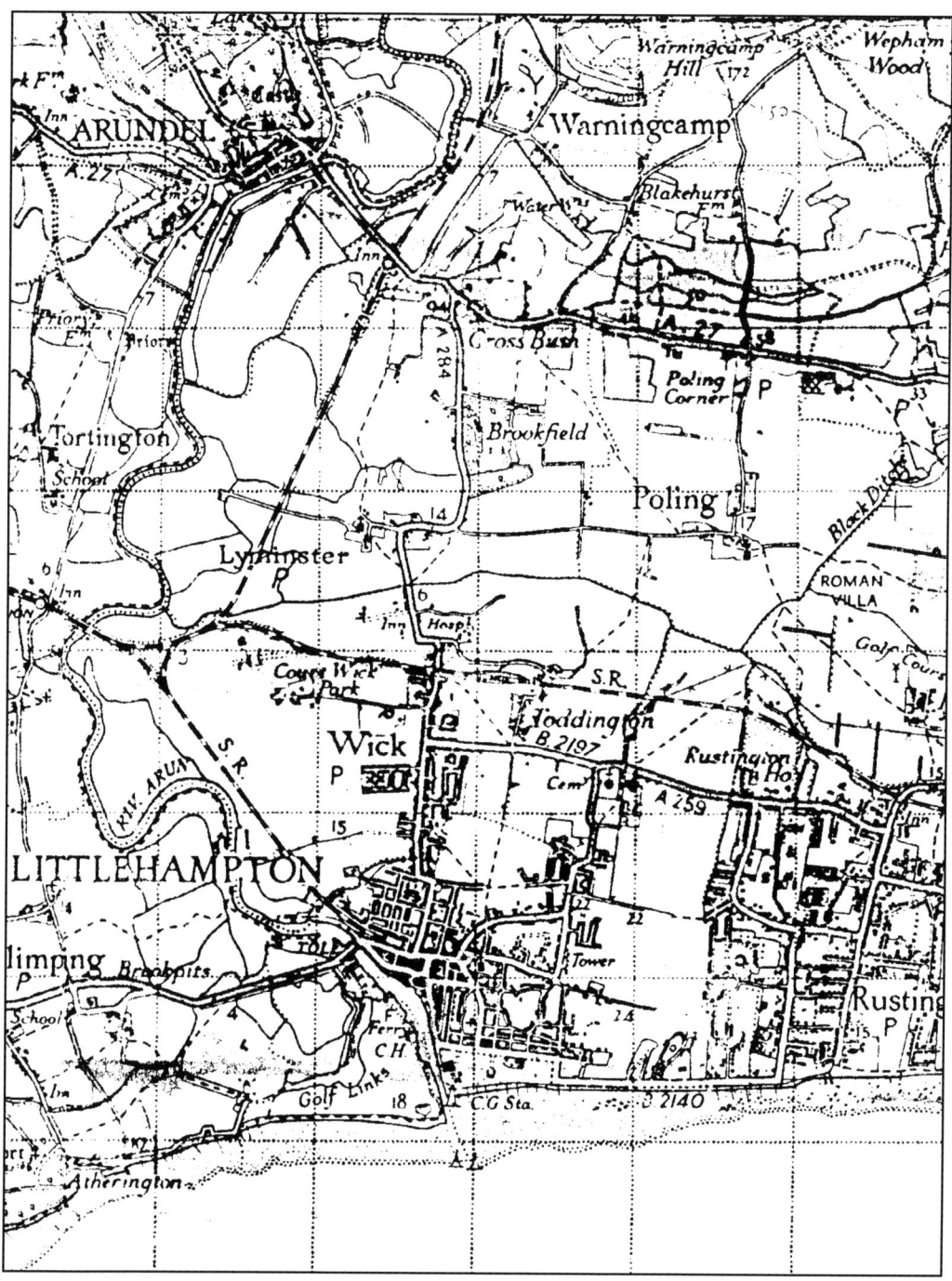

111. PT JUMNA and tow, Littlehampton, 1900s

The iron hulled paddle tug *Jumna* 51grt/1884 would provide towage services at the port for some thirty years, assisting sailing ships entering or leaving or desirous of a tow up to Arundel. In the photograph she is about to drop the tow of a barquentine, which appears to be in no hurry to set sails. *Jumna* always sported a ridiculously long topmast which seems to only have been used for her owner's flag display, or bunting if engaged in tripper trips out to sea. The latter occupation no doubt helped financially when ship tows were a bit thin on the ground. The use of paddle tugs as excursion vessels was not uncommon around the English coasts but regulations hastened the end of such adventures. A blackboard leaning against the West Pier woodwork here at Littlehampton is advertising boat trips, but the crowd look far too well dressed for such.

112. SL PRINCE EDDIE 1900s.
Probably the one and only excursion steamer built at Littlehampton, the 69grt/b1903 built wooden hulled screw propelled vessel was really of a type better suited to the sheltered waters of the Solent. By 1909 she was operating for the Bournemouth and South Coast Steam Packet Company, and in that year again moved to the Ryde Steamboat Company. For whatever reason, she was sold again at the end of the 1909 season, this time to Spain. The ship's 'conning position' is interesting as it largely consists of a steering wheel and compass binnacle, shared with two lifeboats. However substantial canvas awnings and a below deck after saloon afforded reasonable accommodation and protection for the Edwardian trippers - sun and soot free.

113. Holiday crowds line the Arun c1910
A busy holiday scene indeed includes an Indian wigwam and large crowds on both banks of the Arun. PS *Worthing Belle* is raising steam over at Nelson Steps ready to proceed to sea and just visible at her normal out of service berth , is *Jumna*.

114. A motor launch for Arundel c1930

One of Littlehampton's very large open motor boats is seen well laden here setting off upstream probably for Arundel Castle, some seven miles as the river flows. In the distance far left is the famous old shipyard once operated by Harveys who built many fine ocean sailing trading ships. The swing bridge built in 1908 can just be made out with the Railway Wharf wooden piling visible beyond. The bridge was replaced further upstream with a fixed, modern, more traffic friendly structure, by 1980.

115. Tripper motor boats moored c1930
Dating similarly to No.114, several more open motor boats here await their patrons. The River Arun rises some miles east of Horsham in St.Leonards forest, and by the time it reaches the sea is one of England's faster flowing tidal rivers. The constrained entrance is particularly narrow and a shallow bar virtually dries at low water. On the exposed west side efforts appear frequently necessary to maintain the pier groyne. The beaches in this part of West Sussex are generally of sand and safe for bathers, and do not seem to be plagued by the shingle drift so prevalent further east. Apart from river boat trips, in fine weather the motor launches would take trippers out to sea around the Winter Knoll Buoy.

116. The Viking longship replica 'HUGIN'

This fine image ought really to have been placed earlier in the book in the context of boat and ship construction, ie - between Nos 26 and 27. However, since the *Hugin* was definitely photographed entering Littlehampton around 1949, it seems satifactory to include it here. The longboat type evolved over a millennium in Northern Europe, and is probably best known for the Viking invasions prior to 1066. The replica craft shown here was built after WW2 in Norway along the lines of the famous Gokstad ship discovered in 1880. She is entering the River Arun on a promotional round Britain goodwill tour. Rigging for the single mast and square sail was minimal and as the banks of oars are stowed along with the 'warriors' shields on the bulwarks, *Hugin* is part sailing, part drifting in on the tide. Some thirty two shields per side would indicate a theoretical sixty four warrior capability. Dimensions of the vessel were- 79ft. by 17ft with propulsion by sail or sixteen pairs of oars. Rudders had yet to be invented and a large single steering oar can just be seen out on the traditional starboard side aft. Ornate wood carvings decorated bow and stern with the grandest always at the prow. Draught would be very shallow to enable access into creeks, rivers and for beach landings. Cargo carrying versions would have been beamier and deeper.

117. HUGIN's final Kent resting place

The replica *Hugin* duly became a 'monument' commemorating 1,500 years since Hengist's 449A.D. arrival in Britain. In 1949, H.H. Prince Georg of Denmark visited Ebbsfleet, Pegwell Bay to unveil a plaque where the vessel sits on a plinth. This image dates from about 1960.

118. MV SUAVITY, Railway Wharf, Littlehampton

This site developed when the London Brighton & South Coast Railway's branch arrived in 1863. Initially it was used for steam packet services to the Channel Islands and France. Regular services moved east to Newhaven around 1878 leaving the wharf to handle cargo only, a major part of which would have been coal. In this late 1960s photograph just one dock side electric crane remains to unload the ships to waiting rail trucks. Everard's motor coaster *Suavity* 946grt./b1946 is unloading whilst sitting aground at low water. The wharves were later extended and still witness visiting ships in the aggregate trades.

Local Map No.11
Bognor Regis area
(1) Felpham Sluice

9. Seaside health benefits. Resort origins

The popularity of coastal resorts began to grow in the 1730s and inland 'spa' towns became aware of competition. By the 1750s sea bathing (and even the drinking of warm sea water!) were deemed health beneficial and recommended to the population at large. The next century would see yachting, rowing, sea angling and the arrival of piers, boat and paddle steamer trips and that Victorian fascination of 'promenading'. Mass yachting, boat owning, wind, kite and board surfing, plus diving would all later appear, mainly in the last few decades of the 20th century.

Hastings had relied pre 1820 mainly on the local fishing industry, boat and ship construction. At around this time the fashionable Marine Parade began to be constructed steadily westwards along the seafront. Hotels and guest houses proliferated to accommodate the growing numbers of visitors, especially following the 1852 arrival of the railway. The Old Town suffered occasional storm damage as in the 1880s and some poverty existed in that area until WW1. Fortunately, the fishing community stood its ground in the face of change and now welcomes fascinated tourists to what is the last major beach-launched fishing industry base in England.

St. Leonards has become a continuation of Hastings sea front and developed similarly with its own pier, yet when founded in the 1820s by James Burton, it had been a 'green fields' site down to the sea.

Bexhill's origins go back much further, but it would be the De La Warrs' influence from the 1870s that would shape the resort we see today. The art-deco style Pavilion forms the centre piece along the seafront where no pier ever materialised.

Eastbourne is thought to have been a fishing hamlet from Roman times and it did appear in the Domesday book. By 1801 a recorded population of 1,668 souls dwelt in two hundred and forty three homes. In the 1930s some 60,000 lived here. The town's benefactors were the Dukes of Devonshire, particularly the 7th Duke from around 1834. His planning and action as the town's Landlord paved the way for growth and prosperity in the Borough.

Seaford, that most westerly of the Old Cinque Ports, lost its maritime importance from 1539 as we have already seen, when the River Ouse shifted to Newhaven. Today Seaford is a quiet residential town still with a largely unspoilt seafront.

Brighton is thought to have had a Roman settlement but its exposed location and susceptibility to storm damage would hold back its development for centuries. The arrival in 1756 of Dr. Richard Russell became pivotal in the resurrection of the place. He recommended bathing in sea water to aid recovery from various ailments and diseases. Visitors and money began to flow into Brighton much aided by Royal Patronage in 1783 by the then Prince of Wales (later George IV). Apart from the gentrification, money was actually spent on building proper sea walls to minimise inundations and Brighton as a resort has never looked back.

Worthing town came into existence in the late 1700s partially as a result of trouble abroad preventing the gentry from taking their grand tours of Europe. In 1797 the Prince Regent's sister Princess Amelia stayed in the town and a succession of Queens, Dukes and Earls are said to have had residencies in or close around the Worthing area shortly thereafter. The benefits of seaside activity and that movement freedom given to the Public by the railways saw Worthing's population develop steadily, as the town grew into a less brash version of its eastern neighbour across the bay.

Bognor's small fishing hamlet became the site in 1787 for Sir Richard Hotham's proposed health destination. He had been Parliamentarian for the London Borough of Southwark and purchased an old farmhouse and 1,600 acres of land at Bognor. He made the farmhouse into his 'Bognor Lodge' and endeavoured to obtain Royal patronage for his venture. This appears at first to have somewhat eluded him, but Princess Charlotte did visit and approve. Part of early Bognor now resides beneath the waves, and it would not be until 1928 that 'Regis' would be added to the name after King George V's period of local convalescence following serious illness.

119. ANNIE, working cargo, Bognor beach

Here we see the ketch *Annie* 64r/1875 and built locally by Harvey's of Littlehampton, sitting on the beach working cargo from horses and carts in time honoured manner. The scene had been thought to be one of coal unloading, which happened opposite Lennox Street just east of the pier. Judging by the apparent cleanliness of a cart and white dust spilled down the ship's leeboard, it is probable that she was loading a flour cargo. In 1876, nearby Pagham Harbour closed to all shipping as a result of land reclamation, and it is quite likely that cargoes to and from the large Sidlesham Mill may have been diverted to Bognor. Also, after the 1864 railway arrival in the town little coal would have come in by sea. The ketch has the traditional cargo boom rigged with block and tackle to haul sacks onboard. Bognor was never an easy place to approach from seaward since the long line of Bognor rocks lay not far offshore. The tips of these are uncovered at low water and may just be made out ahead of the ship. Hawsers can be seen holding the ship in position when afloat and the forward one will assist duly in hauling off to sea.

120. PS PRINCESS → MAY, Bognor Pier c1900

This 263grt, 1893 built paddler belonged to the Brighton, Worthing and South Coast Steamboat Company. In the photograph she is just setting off from the pier with a good load of trippers. Campbell's bought this ship and *Brighton Belle* in 1901 but sold *Princess May* in 1902. They really never needed to remove the modest wheelhouse - but nevertheless did so!

121. Bognor Pier's heyday →

Yes, it's the *Worthing Belle* again at the western end of her territory, about one hundred years ago. Bognor Pier was a far more modest arrangement than many of those to the east, yet it still attracted the trippers and promenaders just the same. A good flotilla of small boats are moored just offshore, so the weather must have been settled. *Worthing Belle's* stoker is having a break before sailing!

122. SHAMROCK - Bognor 1912 regatta

Rowing and sailing regattas were extremely popular in Victorian and Edwardian times and here we see the little clinker built boat *Shamrock* of Bognor proudly exhibiting a winning certificate. The boatmen are left, Joseph Raglass, right, George Robinson Raglass and in the boat, Walter Scott Raglass, all well known local boatmen and fishermen. The delightful little clinker built boat sports an unusually long jib boom at a jaunty angle. Judging by the calm sea and barely fluttering pendant, going anywhere fast that day was not going to be an option. Bognor's fishermen specialised in lobsters, crabs and prawns according to season, the rough ground off Selsey Bill being ideal for large lobsters which would be caught in beehive shaped wicker pots with a top opening. These would be ballasted down by flints

123. MB SILVER SPRAY →

It is summer time around 1930 and a pair of white hulled motor boats are engaged in Bognor's beach tripper trade. The nearest boat is carvel hulled, smooth sided as opposed to the traditional clinker variety, and both craft have been freshly painted for their summer pursuit. Again, the very large Union flag and pendants flying seem to indicate a further lack of wind on this day.

124. Bognor's truncated pier in 2009 →

From its earlier glory days the pier has suffered from storms and the passage of time generally. Until recently, a few extra hundred feet of pier structure played host to the annual Bognor Birdman Rally with intrepid individuals attempting, in fancy dress and ever more elaborate human powered devices, to 'fly' or glide some 100 metres before crashing into the sea, in the vain hope of winning a prize. Most dropped straight off the pier into the sea. This fun event has been held at Worthing lately, as Bognor Pier shrank ever further shorewards. Just visible still in the distance are the ever menacing line of Bognor rocks, still waiting to catch the unwary mariner.

125. OWERS Light Vessel 1960s
This makes an interesting comparison to the earlier type seen on station at the Royal Sovereign. This light ship is representative of the final manned version in the Trinity House fleet. Some of these craft would later lose their after mast in deference to providing an area suitable for helicopter landing for the maintenance men, following full un-manned automation. Further examples such as the Owers would duly be replaced by large, high focal plane light buoys. The Owers some seven miles offshore, is still a vital seamark for ships entering the Solent and wishing to avoid the foul ground off Selsey Bill. Our book journey westwards has ended.

Local Map No.12
Selsea and Pagham Harbour (1830s)
(1) Sidlesham Mill

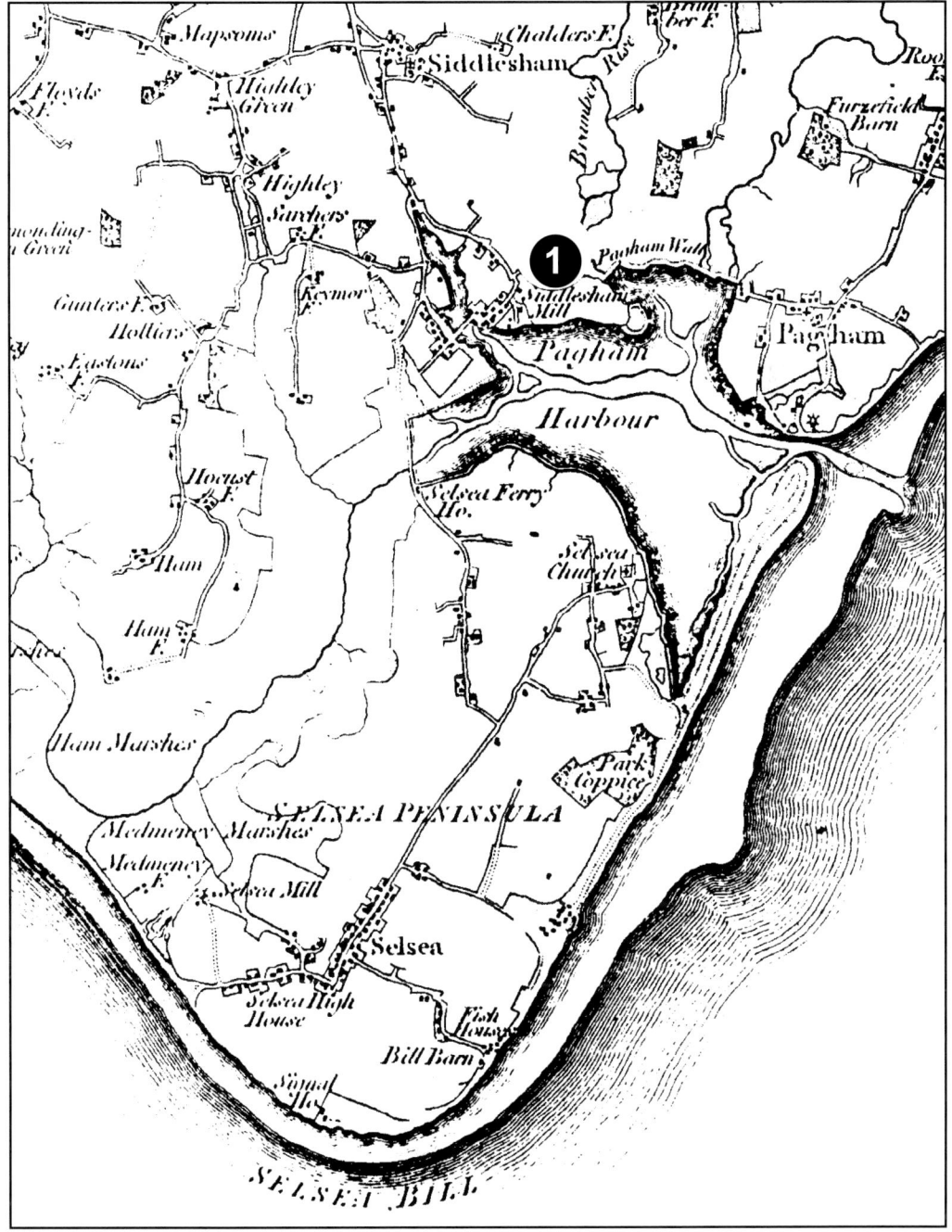

Local Map No.13
Selsey and Pagham Harbour (1948)
(1) Pagham Harbour largely reclaimed and channels abandoned

10. Proposed harbour schemes. Modern marinas.

Proposed harbour schemes

Hastings

In the early 1800s, after years of cross-Channel animosity, trade began to flourish. The well known engineer, John Rennie devised a harbour scheme that would have enclosed an inner wet dock basin by way of outer breakwaters. Estimated costs proved prohibitive and nothing transpired. Another scheme was proposed at around the time of the railway's local arrival. The topography at Hastings did not lend itself for rail access to the shoreline.

The 1896/7 proposals by Carey for a large breakwater harbour with working berths along each arm and a central dock, were at least feasible and partially implemented, although subsequently abandoned in short order. His ambitious plan envisaged a 295 yard eastern breakwater arm, a 450 yard curving western breakwater encompassing a 24 acre inner dock basin. When construction of the western arm became quite advanced, a seemingly intractable problem arose concerning settlement of foundations into a deep mud filled sea bed gully, thought to have been an old river bed course. Ultimate abandonment of the project occurred in part due to opposition locally, and a lack of funds. Curiously though, the structure that had been completed would prove its worth in retaining shingle drift, thereby building a larger more useful beach and providing much more shelter for Hastings' fishing fleet operations. Today's area of amusements and the miniature railway reside on this gained land. See page 150 for the Hastings Harbour plan.

St.Leonards

In the 1830s James Burton put forward a modest proposal for a breakwater harbour design, again with inner and outer areas encompassed by two 400ft piers. Funding failed to materialise and neither did the harbour.

Eastbourne

A small scheme arose in 1893 to provide a protective harbour for the import of gasworks coal. Quite possibly this was conceived as a ploy to make the London, Brighton and South Coast Railway reduce their tariffs for moving coal from Newhaven docks by rail, to Eastbourne. The rail movement of coal would continue in the same manner until 1966.

Brighton

In 1806 a plan, never to be executed, proposed a breakwater style harbour directly opposite East Street and West Street from the beach. Two 800ft arms would have enclosed a 14 acre wet basin surrounded by warehouses. Brighton's ever more fashionable seafront area folk had already objected to coal traffic from the unloading of colliers on the beach, and did not relish the thoughts of more goods traffic to and from the proposed warehouses. The project was doomed!

In any case the beach coal trade moved to Shoreham by around 1830 and presumably the merchants' carts turned inland from the coast road before they reached fashionable areas.

About 1843 yet another very grandiose scheme designed by Captain J.N.Taylor came to light, and is partially explained under image No.73. Some 95 open, timber framed floating sections would be anchored to the sea bed to form swell reducing breakwaters each to have been 84ft in length and 26ft high. Three trial sections were actually built and put afloat in 1845. The customary Channel storms soon sent them ashore! There were also another two or three dubious schemes waiting in the wings, but to no avail, Shoreham Harbour's Southwick to Aldrington Canal became fully operational from 1855.

There appears to have been little interest in harbour projects along the more sparsely populated West Sussex coast.

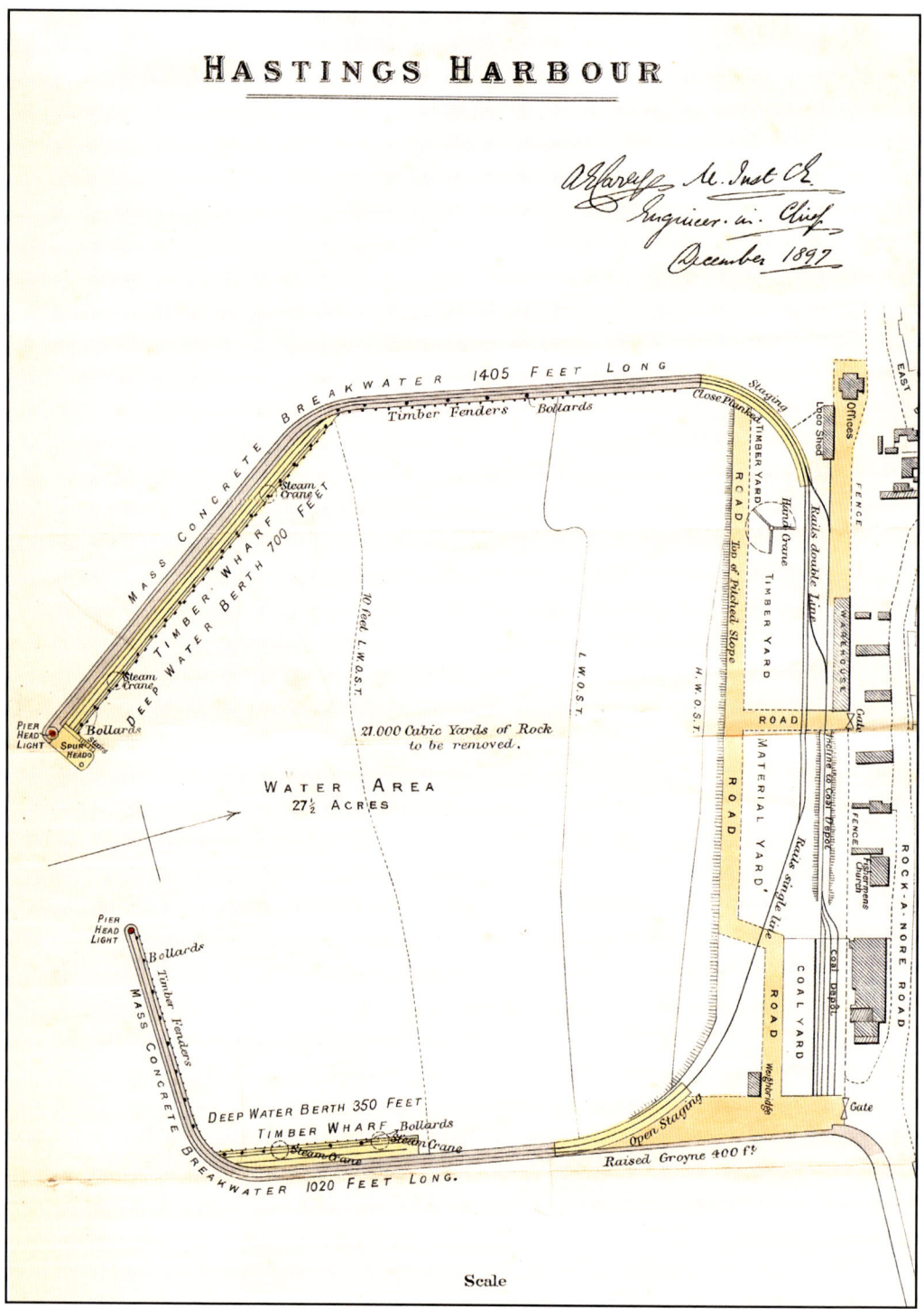

Modern Marinas

Sovereign Harbour

The last big coastal marina to be constructed in Sussex opened in 1993 at Langney Point just east of Eastbourne on the old Crumbles area, and it is still evolving. The site is quite vast, well planned and laid out. A network of yacht basins are interconnected with walkways surrounding, and attractive cross bridges. Residential blocks are set back from the basin edges and road access serves the rear of the properties, making the whole project pedestrian friendly. There are shops, offices, boat repair facilities, chandlery, restaurants and the customary tourist attractions available. Access to and from the sea is via two large sea locks and a curving entrance channel cut through the shingle. An original Martello tower makes a good navigational seamark for visiting craft - the opposite of its original 1806 purpose! See image captions for more.

Brighton Marina

Effectively created by seriously heavy engineering in the 1970s, this project would succeed against the old enemy of Channel storms. Completed around 1980 it has become a popular yachting/ leisure/ tourist and residential area with housing, shops, offices, cinema, car parks etc; now branded as the Marina Village. See image captions for construction detail.

APPENDICES

Sussex beach built vessels extant 1873
from: SUSSEX PORTS SHIPPING DIRECTORY

Year Built	Name	Reg.Tons	Type	Built at:	Notes:
1841	BETSY	23	Sloop	Hastings	Last trading vessels built, owned
1832	COLONEL EVANS	24	Cutter	"	and registered at Hastings
1838	PELICAN	97	Brig	"	" "
1838	PHOENIX	74	Ketch	"	" "
1843	THOMAS&WILLIAM	23	Sloop	"	" "
1840	WANDERER	114	Schooner	"	" "

Year Built	Name	Reg.Tons	Type	Built at:	Notes:
1865	ALBERTINE *	18	Yacht	Hastings	* A second ALBERTINE was
1845	BEE	19	Fishing/	"	built in 1885 and another NEW
1866	BRITISH QUEEN	29	Luggers	"	ALBERTINE appeared in 1891
1847	CHARLOTTE	18	"	"	(All tripper boats/yachts)
1846	FAME	18	"	"	
1869	FANNY	25	"	"	
1860	FAVORITE	26	"	"	
1858	FAWN	22	"	"	Small to medium sized fishing
1846	GODILD	19	"	"	boats of wooden construction
1857	HAPPY RETURN	26	"	"	continued to be built at Hastings
1845	IDAS	17	"	"	until after WW2. By 1980 such
1859	JANE	21	"	"	methods had ceased.
1845	MARGARET&ELIZABETH	17	"	"	
1847	NORDSTERN	24	"	"	
1847	OCEAN QUEEN	20	"	"	
1860	PARAGON	23	"	"	
1845	SARAH&FRANCIS	18	"	"	
1847	SWAN	30	"	"	
1857	THOMAS&ELIZABETH	17	"	"	
1862	THREE SISTERS	27	"	"	
1857	WILLIAM&ELIZA	24	"	"	

(Vessels of less than 10-15 tons were not recorded in the Directory)

Year Built	Name	Reg.Tons	Type	Built at:	Notes:
1858	BARBARA	18	"	Eastbourne	
1847	FAVORITE	20	"	"	
					The following craft were recorded in Henry Cheal's 1909 'Ships & Mariners of Shoreham'
1834	CRITERION	17-25 Tons	"	Brighton	
1835	RAMBLER	"	"	"	
1835	RANGER	"	"	"	
1835	CAROLINE	"	"	"	
1835	MYSTERY	"	"	"	
1836	KITTY	"	"	"	
1845	DUKE OF WELLINGTON	"	"	"	
1833	PEARL	"	"	Hove	
1845	CAROLINE	"	"	"	

I. Sussex beach built vessels extant in 1873

Sussex registered vessels extant 1873
Statistics from the 'SUSSEX PORTS SHIPPING DIRECTORY'
Some added notes:

Type	Nos.	Reg.Tons	Notes: Where built.
Port of Shoreham			
Steamers ^	3	1,341	
Brigs	68	16,112	Shoreham : 50
Barques	38	13,129	Shoreham : 21; Littlehampton: 4; Rye : 1
Brigantines & Schooners	18	2,578	Shoreham : 10
Sloops, Yawls and Ketches	9	462	Shoreham : 4
Fishing Vessels & Yachts	*22	423	Var. Shoreham, Hove, Worthing, Newhaven
Vessels hailing from other ports	6	876	
Totals	**164**	**34,921**	

* Many vessels less than 15 tons unlisted
^ Incl. 1 Tug; 2 Cargo Steamers

Port of Littlehampton			
Barques	11	3,429	Littlehampton : 4
Brigs	9	1,483	Arundel ; 1; Shoreham : 1
Brigantines & Schooners	15	1,602	Littlehampton : 4; Emsworth : 1
Ketches, etc	8	866	Littlehampton : 2; Emsworth : 1; Bosham :1
Fishing Vessels & Yachts	16	380	Var. L'ton, Arundel, Bosham & Emsworth
Vessels hailing from other ports	1	572	
Totals	**60**	**7,832**	
Port of Newhaven			
Steamers #	8	1,287	
Barque	1	170	Newhaven
Brigs	12	2,236	Newhaven : 1; Rye : 2
Brigantines & Schooners	4	513	Lewes : 3
Fishing Vessels & Yachts	11	208	Var. Newhaven, Lewes, Eastbourne & Rye
Totals	**36**	**4,414**	

\# Incl. 1 Tug; 7 Cross Channel Steamers.

Port of Rye with Hastings			
Barque	1	289	
Brigs	8	1,206	Littlehampton : 1; Hastings : 1
Brigantines	10	1,328	Rye ; 2
Schooners	27	2,623	Rye : 13 ; Hastings : 1
Ketches, Dandies etc. *	14	645	Rye : 3 ; Hastings : 4
Fishing Vessels & Yachts>	31	699	Rye : 6; Hastings : 21
Totals	**91**	**6,790**	

* Includes Sloops, Cutters, etc.
A 'Dandie' resembled a sloop of unusual rig.
> 164 Fishing Vessels less than 10 tons unlisted

Grand Totals	**351**	**53,957**	

General note
The building of wooden hulled, deep sea trading merchant sailing ships ceased in Sussex around 1880. Wooden coastal trading ketch construction continued at Rye and Littlehampton just into the 20th Century. Littlehampton turned out the last of the type in 1919.

II. Sussex registered vessels extant in 1873

Trading areas for Sussex ships in 1873

When examined in detail, the 'snapshot' analysis for the year shows a period of great overseas trading activity for Sussex owned merchant ships. Steamers had yet to make any real impression on local ship owners, and indeed wooden hulled cargo carriers continued to descend Shoreham's slipways for a further seven years. Iron and steel hulled vessels never would.

The main long distance traders of the day would have been the square rigged barques and brigs, and fore and aft sailed schooners. The more simply rigged barquentines and brigantines were growing in popularity due to their easier manning requirements. Such craft nevertheless, averaged between 250 to perhaps 600 tons cargo capacity, which in modern times seems miniscule indeed. A few brigantines and schooners continued to hang on until WW1 in the coastal coal and Baltic timber trades, but the steamers would conquer universally with their own replacement type, the motor ship, being but a few years over the horizon.

By 1880 trade patterns had changed and the age old cargo handling methods on Sussex beaches would pass into history. Ships generally were becoming larger and more expensive to insure and operate. Proper harbour facilities were now a necessity.

The last wooden sailing coasters in any numbers were the West Country schooners and ketches some continuing to eke out a living often with auxiliary motor power, until the 1950s.

In 1873:-
34 Shoreham vessels were trading Worldwide.
17 " " to the Mediterranean
13 " " to Northern Europe/Baltic Sea
29 " " Coastwise

9 Littlehampton " Worldwide
1 " " to the Mediterranean
3 " " to Northern Europe/Baltic Sea
27 " " Coastwise

3 Newhaven " to the Baltic Sea
14 " " Coastwise

4 Rye * " Worldwide
1 " " to the Mediterranean
2 " " to Northern Europe/Baltic Sea
49 " " Coastwise

(* Rye figures include Hastings)

III. Trading areas for Sussex ships in 1873

Sailing rigs on the Sussex Coast 1800-1900

 Trading Smack 1800	 Beach Yawl 1880	 Ketch 1890
 Topsail Schooner 1840	 Brig or Snow* 1860	 Brigantine 1890
 Topsail Schooner 1870	 Barque 1860	 Barquentine 1870
 Fishing Lugger 1850	 Fishing Lugger 1900	

Notes:
Dates indicative of rig type popularity only.
Brigs and Barques were often simply rigged down to Brigantines and Barquentines for ease of handling by smaller crews.
*Snow type same as Brig but with the addition of a small extra mast close abaft the mainmast for the 'spanker' sail.

IV. Sailing rigs on the Sussex coast (1800-1900)

Bibliography

Title	Author	Year	ISBN
Ships and Mariners of Shoreham	Henry Cheal	1909 (reprint 1981)	0 9507 5711 X
Old Ship Prints	E.Keble Chatterton	1927	-
A History of the Southern Railway	F.Dendy Marshall	1936	-
Ports of the United Kingdom	Sir David J. Owen	1939	-
British Paddle Steamers	Geoffrey Body	1971	0 7153 5118 4
South Eastern Sail	Michael Bouquet	1972	0 7153 5592 9
Victorian & Edwardian Sussex - in old photographs	James B.Gray	1973	0 7340 0131 1
The Seaborne Trade of Sussex	John Farrant	1976 *	
The Harbours of Sussex	John Farrant	1976 *	

* Sussex Archaeological Society, Lewes. Historical papers

Title	Author	Year	ISBN
A Maritime History of Rye	John Collard	1978	0 9506 2762 3
Stephenson Clarke	Craig J.M.Carter	1981	0 9056 1717 7
Gas and Electricity Colliers	D.Ridley Chesterton & R.S.Fenton	1984	0 9056 1733 9
Smuggling in Kent & East Sussex	Mary Waugh	1984	0 9053 9248 5
Fishermen of Hastings	Steve Peak	1985	0 9510 7060 6
Kent & East Sussex Waterways	P.A.L.Vine	1989	0 9065 2072 X
The Steam Collier Fleets	J.A.MacRae & C.V.Waine	1990	0 9051 8412 2
The Sussex Weather Book	Bob Ogley, Ian Currie, Mark Davison	1991	0 8723 3730 9
Rye Shipping Memories	Richard Horner	1993	1 8706 0017 7
Maritime Sussex	David Harris	1997	1 8577 0122 4
Coastal and Short Sea Liners	C.V.Waine	1999	0 9051 8417 3
P.&A. Campbell Pleasure Steamers	C.Collard	1999	0 7524 1711 8
Byegone Rye Harbour (Rye Memories)	Jo Kirkham (Ed.)	2006	1 8706 0025 8
Hastings, St.Leonards & Eastbourne Steam boat Company	David Renno	2008	-
Lloyds Registers	-	Var.	-
Mercantile Navy Lists	-	Var.	—

Index

(Ship and boat names in CAPITALS, places and subjects in lower case)

ADUR	122	Palace	100	F.E.WEBB	116
Adur, River	108	West	102,107	FOREST BELLE	124
ADVENTURE	74	BRIGHTON QUEEN	58	Freedom of individuals	92
ALACRITY	48	BRITANNIA (beach yacht)	48,49	FRESHWATER	56
ALBERTINE (1) & (2)	48,77,152	BROADHURST (1)	113,114	Gasworks	92,109-114
ALBION	81	BROMELIA	12	GERMANIA	68
Aldrington Basin	86			GLEN GOWER	81
ALEXANDRA (b.1863)	37	CARBONARIA	112	GOLDEN CITY	48
ALEXANDRA (b.1879)	118	CARRICK CASTLE	58	GOODWILL	74
ALGEIBA	113, 118	Chalk/Lime Trade	66	GREYHOUND	72
ALGOL	113	Chichester, Port of	10,11,111	GULNARE	34
ALICE V.GOODHUE	113, 114	Cinque Ports, the	9		
ALLEYN	59	CLIFF QUAY	120	HAWK	22
AMBERLEY	114	Clinker built boats	34	Hastings Pier	21
ANNIE	142	Coal, the long 'reign' of	109	Hastings, St.Leonards &	
ANTARES	112	'Coal Whippers'	47	Eastbourne Steamboat Co	37
ARCTURUS	112	COLONEL EVANS	152	Heene	11
med Lugger, an	16	COMMERCE	78,112	HENRY MOON	113,114
ARTHUR WRIGHT	113	CONFLICT	112,113,114	'Hog boats'	97
ARUNDEL	122	CONSUL	83	Holywell Quarry	61
Arundel, Port of	11	Cow Gap	64	Hove	
Arun, River	132-138	Crumbles, The	40,151		34
ASHLEY	113	CRUSADER	15	HUGIN	138
ATHOLE	14	Cuckmere, River	74	HYLTON JOLIFFE	96
AUDREY	59	Customs Ports, old	11		
AURIGA	112	CYNTHIA	38	IONA	74
				ISABEL	34
		DOROTHY MELINDA	29		
BALMORAL	59,129-131	DUCHESS OF YORK	39	JAMES JOICEY	78
Beach handled cargoes	65	DUKE OF DEVONSHIRE	83	JAMES ROWAN	122
Beach Sailing Yachts	48	DULWICH	122	JOHN BULL	112
Beachy Head Lighthouse	68			JOHN MILES	114
BEE	34	EARL OF WINDSOR	12	JUMNA	133,135
Belle Tout Lighthouse	70-71	EASTBOURNE BELLE	48		
BETSEY	152	EBERNEZER	112,113,114	KENRIX	113
BETSWOOD	113	ECLIPSE	96	KEYNES	82
Bognor Pier	143,145	ELEANOR BROOKE	118	Kingston Lighthouse	114
Boulder boats & blue flints	65,77	Electricity Works	86,92,109-114		
Brede, River	9	EMPRESS	66	LADY BRASSEY	37
Brighton Beach	93	Ems, River	11	LADY EVELYN	28
BRIGHTON BELLE	28	ENCHANTRESS (1) & (2)	48,50	LADY ROWENA	59
Brighton Marina	102-107,151	ENDEAVOUR	12	LAMBURN	34
Brighton Piers-				Langney Point	40
Chain	96	FAME	12		
		FAVORITE	98		

LESRIX	113	PRINCE EDDIE	134	Smuggling	72
LEVERINGTON	112	PRINCESS MAY	58,142	SOUTHAMPTON	59
Lewes	11	PRINCESS ROYAL	95	SOUTHERN QUEEN	51
Littlehampton, Port of	111,133-139	Proposed harbours	94,119	Southwick	116,120
		PROSPERO	113	Sovereign Harbour	43,151
London, coasting trade	65	PULBOROUGH	114	St.Leonards Pier	30
LURLINE	34			STORRINGTON	122
LYNTON	59	QUEEN OF THE SOUTH	59	SUAVITY	138
		QUEEN VICTORIA	34	SUPERSEACAT ONE	85
Magnus Volk	87-91	QUENTIN DURWARD	96	SUSSEX BELLE	58
MARIA NIBBE	120			Sussex coal consumption	109
Martello Towers	77	Railways, arrival of	92	Sussex iron industry	65
MARY ELIZA	48	RAVENSWOOD	100	Sussex timber trade	65
MAY	59	Resort, origins	141	SUSSEX MAID	77
Medieval Harbours	9	RESULT	80	SUSSEX QUEEN	50
MERCHANT	112	RHOS COLWYN	58	SWAN II	72
METRIC	122	RNLI JAMES STEPHENS	48	SWANAGE QUEEN	50
Modern Marinas	151	Road, transport	92,93		
MOUNTAINEER	96	ROSE	12	TAFF	58
		ROSEMARY ANN	48	TALBOT	90
NEW ALBERTINE	26	Rother, River	8	TANTALLON CASTLE	58
NEW MOON	19	Rottingdean Pier	87	THOMAS & WILLIAM	152
NEW SKYLARK	26	ROYAL SOVEREIGN Lt.Vsl.	41	Tillingham, River	9
Newhaven, Port of	110	ROYAL SOVEREIGN Lt.Tr.	42	Trading smacks	16,63
		RUNNELSTONE	118	Tripper boats	136,137
		Rye Harbour	15	Tripper market	92
OUR PAM & PETER	30	Rye, Port of	110	TWO BROTHERS	29
Ouse, River	9				
OWERS Light Vessel	146	SARAH	112,113,114	VENTUROUS	118
		SARAH ELGAR	12	VESTA	112
Pagham Harbour	10, 147-148	Seaford	76		
PALINDRA	11	SEAGULL (PS)	21	WANDERER	152
PARIS	78	SEAGULL (SS)	113	WAVERLEY	59,124
PELICAN	20, 112.152	Sea Coal	109	WENDY ANNE	48
PENNINE	112	Seaside health benefits	141	WILLIAM ALLCHORN	43,50
Pevensey Haven	9	Selsey Bill	147	Winchelsea	8,9
PHOENIX	152	SHAMROCK	144	W.J.H.WOOD	120
PHYLWOOD	113	SHOREHAM	113,114	WOOLWICH BELLE	59
Pier History	58	Shoreham, Port of	9,111	Worthing	120
Piers, paddle steamers & promenading	58	Ship and boat construction	34	WORTHING	122
		Shipping Companies, (coal)	111	WORTHING BELLE	59,99,124,135,142
'PIONEER' Sea-car	88-91	Sidlesham Mill	147		
PLYMOUTH BELLE	59	SILVER SPRAY	144	Worthing Pier	125,126
Portslade	116	SIR JOHN SNELL	120		
Portslade Gasworks	116	SIR WILLIAM WALKER	122	YOKEFLEET	113
PORTSLADE (2)	114	SKYLARKs	4,8,99,103	YOUNG FLYING FISH	30

Acknowledgements

I would like to record my thanks and appreciation to all the kind individuals, societies and organisations who with their time, information and material have so helped with the compilation of this book, in particular: Michael Alford, Peter Bailey, Christine and Peter Bentley, Sarah Cooper, Zoe Edwards, Esme Evans, John Farrant, Beverley Green, Alison Hawkins, David Jennings, Jenny Lund, Doreen Miller, Phil Neumann, Joe Seaman, Tony Smith, Jill Tucker, Camilla Webster, David Whiteside and Trevor Wolford.

Photographic sources

Michael Alford 3; Bognor Regis Local History Society & Museum 119,120,122; Fotoflite 32,65,95,125; Hastings Public Libraries (Hastings Reference Library) 4,8,9,10,30; Hastings Museum and Art Gallery 11,12; Judges Postcards Ltd 16,17; Newhaven Local and Maritime Historical Society 60,62; The Royal Pavilion and Museums, Brighton and Hove 72,73,74; Towner, Eastbourne 50; West Sussex County Council Library Service 103,104; World Ship Society Photo Library 28,29,46,63,96.

Ordnance Survey maps are from 1930s one inch to one mile scale originals.

Easebourne Lane, Midhurst, West Sussex. GU29 9AZ
Telephone: 01730 813169   Fax: 01730 812601
Email: info@middletonpress.co.uk   www.middletonpress.co.uk

Michael Langley
Solent - Creeks, Craft & Cargoes
South West Harbours - Ships & Trades
Sussex Shipping - Sail, Steam & Motor
Trident Tankers Ltd - A change of course
Kent Seaways - Hoys to Hovercraft

--- *Other Sussex Books* ---

London to Portsmouth Waterway
Battle over Sussex 1940
Blitz over Sussex 1941-42
Bombers over Sussex 1943-45
Bognor at War 1939-45
Defending Sussex Beaches 1940-42
Military Defence of West Sussex
Military Signals from the South Coast
Secret Sussex Resistance
Sussex Home Guard
Betwixt Petersfield & Midhurst
Changing Midhurst
Cowdray and Easebourne
Fernhurst Cylinders
Roman Roads of Sussex

RAILWAY ALBUMS

Branch Lines of Midhurst
Branch Line to Selsey
Crawley to Littlehampton
Haywards Heath to Seaford
Three Bridges to Brighton
Tonbridge to Hastings
Brighton to Eastbourne
Brighton to Worthing
Chichester to Portsmouth
Hastings to Ashford
Worthing to Chichester

see - www.middletonpress.co.uk for further details

or contact us for a brochure listing over 480 titles covering
Local History, Railways, Tramway, Trolleybus and Military